From Idea to

Empire

Mastering the Online Agency

Game

Aniket More

From Idea to Empire

Mastering the Online Agency Game

Aniket More

Published by: Aniket More

Publisher Address: Flat No 302, Prisha Apartment, Virat Hanuman Nagar, Near Raksha Hospital, Ausa Road, Latur - 413512

Printed in India
Edition: 1

ISBN 9798874292317

www.aniketmore.in
connect@aniketmore.in

Disclaimer:

The information provided in this book, "From Idea to Empire: Mastering the Online Agency Game," is intended for educational and informational purposes only. The content within this publication is based on research, industry knowledge, and experiences shared within the digital business landscape up until the book's publication date.

Readers are encouraged to use the information provided as a guide and not as a substitute for professional advice. The success of starting or running an online agency is influenced by various factors including individual dedication, market conditions, and evolving industry standards.

The author and publishers of this book do not guarantee specific outcomes or results from implementing the strategies, recommendations, or information presented within. Every entrepreneurial journey is unique, and while the content aims to provide insights and guidance, individual results may vary.

Additionally, external links, references, or information pertaining to third-party tools, services, or platforms provided in this book are for informational purposes. Readers are advised to conduct their own research and due diligence before making any decisions or investments based on third-party information.

The author, publisher, and affiliated parties are not liable for any direct or indirect consequences or damages resulting from the use or misuse of the information provided within this book.

Readers are urged to consult with relevant professionals, industry experts, or advisors for personalized guidance tailored to their specific circumstances and business needs.

By reading this book, you acknowledge and agree to the terms of this disclaimer.

Table of Contents

Section 6: Simplifying Complexities with Cutting-Edge Automation and Expertise

Chapter 1: The Power of Automation in Digital Business

Chapter 2: ChatGPT Technology and Its Applications in Marketing

Chapter 3: Mastering Lead Generation with Automation

Chapter 4: Optimizing Facebook Ads Using Automation Tools

Chapter 5: Streamlining Social Media Automation Strategies

Chapter 6: Leveraging AI in Creative Design and Content Creation

Chapter 7: Personalization and Targeting with Automated Systems

Chapter 8: Data-Driven Decision Making in Automation

Chapter 9: Integrating Automation into Marketing Workflows

Chapter 10: Future Trends and Innovations in Digital Business Automation

Bonus Chapter

Digital Agency Blueprint: 10 Steps to Launch and Grow Your Online Empire

Section 1: Chapter 1
The Digital Revolution

In the annals of human history, few revolutions have been as transformative and pervasive as the digital revolution. It's an era defined not just by technological advancements but by an unprecedented shift in the way we live, communicate, conduct business, and perceive the world. The digital revolution has heralded an age of remarkable connectivity, empowerment, and innovation, reshaping societies and economies on a global scale.

The Dawn of a New Era

The genesis of this revolution can be traced back to the latter part of the 20th century, characterized by the advent of personal computers and the internet. These technological milestones laid the groundwork for an interconnected world, sparking a monumental transformation that continues to evolve rapidly.

Connectivity Redefined

The internet, once a rudimentary network primarily used for academic and military purposes, burgeoned into a vast web connecting billions of people worldwide. It obliterated geographical barriers, enabling instant communication and information exchange across continents. The proliferation of smartphones further catalyzed this interconnectedness, placing the power of the internet into the palms of individuals, perpetually altering the way we interact, learn, and conduct business.

Digital Disruption in Industries
The impact of the digital revolution reverberates across industries. Traditional paradigms were disrupted as new players emerged, unencumbered by conventional limitations. Established businesses grappled with the need to adapt or face obsolescence. From retail to entertainment, healthcare to finance, virtually every sector experienced seismic shifts, redefining consumer behavior, business models, and competitive landscapes.

Unveiling the Digital Business Landscape:
Rise of Online Entrepreneurship
Central to this revolution is the rise of online entrepreneurship. The digital realm has become fertile ground for innovators and visionaries, offering unprecedented opportunities to transform ideas into thriving businesses. The barriers to entry have lowered significantly, enabling virtually anyone with an idea and determination to launch and scale a business online.

Agility and Innovation
One hallmark of the digital age is the emphasis on agility and innovation. Start-ups and agile enterprises thrive in this environment, leveraging technology to pivot swiftly, adapt to market changes, and capitalize on emerging trends. The ability to

innovate has become a cornerstone of success, fostering a culture where experimentation and iteration are celebrated.

Impact on Digital Agencies
The evolution of the digital landscape has profoundly affected the dynamics of digital agencies. These entities serve as catalysts, assisting businesses in navigating the complexities of the online sphere. From web development to digital marketing, they offer specialized services crucial for businesses aiming to establish and expand their digital footprint.

Shifting Paradigms in Agency Services
Digital agencies have transformed from mere service providers to strategic partners, guiding businesses through the intricacies of the digital ecosystem. The scope of their services has expanded, encompassing not only website development but also search engine optimization, content creation, social media management, and data analytics.

Collaborative Ecosystems
Moreover, digital agencies operate within a collaborative ecosystem, forging alliances with technology platforms, influencers, and industry experts. This interconnectedness allows for the seamless integration of cutting-edge tools and expertise, empowering agencies to deliver innovative solutions tailored to their clients' needs.

Looking Ahead
As we stand on the precipice of this digital era, the pace of change shows no signs of abating. Technologies like artificial intelligence, augmented reality, and blockchain are poised to redefine industries yet again, opening new frontiers and possibilities.

The digital revolution is not without its challenges. Privacy concerns, cybersecurity threats, and ethical implications loom large, demanding vigilant and responsible stewardship of these transformative technologies.

Conclusion

In conclusion, the digital revolution has irrevocably altered the fabric of our existence, creating a world interconnected as never before. For businesses and entrepreneurs, it presents boundless opportunities and challenges in equal measure. Understanding and navigating this landscape is imperative for those seeking to thrive in the digital age—an age where adaptability, innovation, and technological prowess reign supreme.

Section 1: Chapter 2
Understanding the Online Business Landscape

In the dynamic realm of online business, success is often contingent upon a comprehensive understanding of the landscape. To navigate this terrain effectively, entrepreneurs must decipher the intricacies, opportunities, and challenges that define the digital marketplace.

The Evolution of Online Business:
Birth of E-Commerce

The inception of e-commerce marked a watershed moment in the business landscape. Amazon's pioneering success and the dot-com boom of the late 1990s catalyzed a shift in consumer behavior, fostering a newfound trust in online transactions. Today, e-commerce is a cornerstone of the digital economy, encompassing a myriad of products and services, from retail to subscription-based models.

Emergence of Diverse Business Models

The online ecosystem has birthed diverse business models beyond e-commerce. Subscription services, Software as a Service (SaaS), the gig economy, digital content creation, and online marketplaces have flourished, offering entrepreneurs multifaceted avenues to explore and capitalize upon.

Key Components of the Online Business Landscape:
Digital Marketing and Branding

In the digital sphere, effective marketing and branding are pivotal. Businesses vie for attention in a crowded online space, necessitating astute marketing strategies that leverage social media, content marketing, SEO, and influencer partnerships to engage and retain customers.

Customer Experience and Engagement

Central to the success of any online venture is the customer experience. With a plethora of options at their fingertips, consumers expect seamless navigation, personalized interactions, and exceptional service. Businesses that prioritize customer satisfaction gain a competitive edge in an increasingly discerning market.

Data Analytics and Insights

Data has emerged as a potent currency in the digital landscape. Analyzing customer behavior, market trends, and performance metrics empowers businesses to make informed decisions, optimize strategies, and tailor offerings to meet evolving demands.

Shifting Consumer Behavior:
Mobile-First Approach

The proliferation of smartphones has propelled a mobile-first approach. Businesses need to optimize their online presence for mobile devices, ensuring a user-friendly experience and capitalizing on the ubiquity of mobile technology.

Rise of Social Commerce

Social media platforms have evolved into vibrant marketplaces, fostering social commerce. Consumers now discover, research, and purchase products directly through platforms like Instagram, Facebook, and TikTok, necessitating a strategic presence on these channels.

Challenges and Opportunities:

Competitive Landscape

The online space is fiercely competitive. Standing out amidst the cacophony of voices requires innovation, differentiation, and a deep understanding of one's target audience.

Cybersecurity Concerns

As businesses move online, cybersecurity threats loom large. Safeguarding customer data and ensuring a secure online environment are paramount to building trust and credibility.

Conclusion

Understanding the multifaceted online business landscape is indispensable for entrepreneurs seeking to establish and expand their digital ventures. It requires a nuanced comprehension of consumer behavior, technological trends, and market dynamics. With a solid grasp of this landscape, entrepreneurs can craft strategic business plans, capitalize on emerging opportunities, and navigate challenges effectively.

Section 1: Chapter 3
Evolution of Digital Agencies

Digital agencies stand as vanguards in the rapidly evolving landscape of online business. These entities have metamorphosed over time, adapting and innovating to meet the dynamic needs of businesses navigating the intricacies of the digital sphere. Understanding the evolutionary journey of digital agencies is crucial for entrepreneurs aspiring to establish successful ventures in this domain.

Genesis of Digital Agencies:
Early Beginnings

Digital agencies trace their roots to the emergence of the internet and the subsequent demand for web development and design services. In the nascent stages, these agencies primarily focused on building websites, reflecting the limited scope of the digital landscape at the time.

Expansion of Services

As the digital ecosystem burgeoned, digital agencies diversified their offerings to encompass a broader spectrum of services. They evolved from singularly focused web development agencies to multidisciplinary entities adept at providing comprehensive digital solutions.

Transformation into Strategic Partners:
Shift in Agency-Client Relationships

The evolution of digital agencies brought about a pivotal shift in their relationships with clients. No longer confined to mere service providers, agencies assumed the role of strategic partners, collaborating with businesses to craft holistic digital strategies aligned with organizational objectives.

Holistic Approach to Digital Solutions

The contemporary digital agency operates under a holistic paradigm, recognizing the interconnectedness of various facets of online business. Services span beyond web development, encompassing digital marketing, SEO, content creation, social media management, data analytics, and more.

Agile and Innovative Practices:
Embracing Agility

Agility lies at the core of successful digital agencies. In an environment characterized by rapid change, these entities embrace agile methodologies, enabling them to pivot swiftly, adapt to emerging trends, and respond to client needs with flexibility and speed.

Culture of Innovation

Innovation permeates the ethos of modern digital agencies. They foster a culture that encourages experimentation, creativity, and constant improvement. This relentless pursuit of innovation enables agencies to stay ahead of the curve and deliver cutting-edge solutions to clients.

Collaborative Ecosystems and Specializations:
Collaborative Partnerships

Digital agencies thrive within collaborative ecosystems. Partnerships with technology providers, content creators, influencers, and industry experts foster an environment of knowledge exchange and mutual growth. Leveraging these networks allows agencies to integrate specialized expertise seamlessly.

Niche Specializations

As the digital landscape expands, agencies often carve out niche specializations to differentiate themselves in a competitive market. Some specialize in specific industries, technologies, or services, offering tailored solutions that cater to unique client needs.

Future Trajectories:
Technology-Driven Future

The future of digital agencies is intertwined with technological advancements. Emerging technologies like artificial intelligence, augmented reality, and blockchain are poised to revolutionize the way agencies deliver services and interact with clients.

Emphasis on Data and Personalization

Data-centric strategies and personalization will drive the future trajectory of digital agencies. Harnessing data insights and leveraging personalization technologies will be instrumental in crafting bespoke solutions that resonate with target audiences.

Conclusion

The evolution of digital agencies mirrors the dynamic evolution of the digital landscape itself. From humble beginnings as web development firms to becoming indispensable strategic partners, these agencies have continuously adapted to the changing demands of the digital era.

Understanding this evolution is pivotal for entrepreneurs aiming to establish and scale online agency businesses. Embracing agility, fostering innovation, nurturing collaborative ecosystems, and staying abreast of technological advancements will be pivotal in navigating the future landscape of digital agencies.

Section 1: Chapter 4
Leveraging Technology for Business Growth

In the fast-evolving landscape of online business, technology stands as a catalyst for growth and innovation. Entrepreneurs who harness the power of cutting-edge technologies within their digital agencies are poised not only to thrive but to redefine the paradigms of success in the digital era.

Technology as a Business Enabler:
Embracing Digital Transformation
Digital agencies at the vanguard of the industry recognize that embracing digital transformation is pivotal. This encompasses the integration of technologies to streamline operations, enhance customer experiences, and drive business growth.

Impact of Emerging Technologies

Technological innovations such as artificial intelligence (AI), machine learning, big data analytics, automation, and the Internet of Things (IoT) have reshaped the landscape of business operations, presenting unprecedented opportunities for growth and optimization.

Transformative Applications of Technology:
AI and Machine Learning

Artificial intelligence and machine learning algorithms are revolutionizing how businesses operate. From predictive analytics to chatbots and personalized customer experiences, AI-powered solutions empower agencies to deliver more efficient and tailored services.

Big Data Analytics

The advent of big data analytics has transformed the way businesses derive insights from vast amounts of data. Analyzing customer behavior, market trends, and operational metrics enables agencies to make data-driven decisions, optimize strategies, and identify growth opportunities.

Automation for Efficiency and Scale:
Streamlining Operations

Automation technologies streamline repetitive tasks, optimizing operational efficiency within digital agencies. Automated workflows, email marketing automation, project management tools, and content scheduling platforms are integral to scaling operations.

Scaling Services

Automation not only enhances efficiency but also facilitates scalability. Digital agencies can deliver services at scale without compromising quality, thereby catering to a broader client base and driving business expansion.

Personalization and Customer-Centricity:
Customization through Technology
Technology enables agencies to craft personalized experiences for clients. Tailoring services based on individual client needs and preferences fosters stronger relationships and client satisfaction, leading to long-term partnerships.

Enhanced Customer Engagement
Digital agencies leverage technology to engage customers across various touchpoints. Whether through interactive websites, targeted email campaigns, or AI-powered chatbots, agencies can create seamless and engaging experiences that resonate with their audience.

Technology Adoption Challenges and Strategies:
Overcoming Resistance
Adopting new technologies often faces resistance. It requires a cultural shift within agencies, encouraging a mindset that embraces change, continuous learning, and experimentation.

Strategic Implementation
Strategic implementation of technology is crucial. Agencies must align technology adoption with their business goals, ensuring that investments in technology yield tangible returns and contribute to business growth.

Future Technological Trajectories:
Evolving Technologies

The future trajectory of technology in digital agencies is promising. Advancements in AI, augmented reality (AR), virtual reality (VR), blockchain, and 5G networks will open up new avenues for innovation and disruption.

Ethical and Responsible Use

As technology continues to evolve, digital agencies must prioritize ethical and responsible use. Data privacy, cybersecurity, and ethical considerations in AI and automation are imperative to build trust and credibility.

Conclusion

Technology serves as the bedrock for digital agency success in the contemporary business landscape. Its transformative potential enables agencies to enhance operations, personalize services, and scale business growth.

Entrepreneurs embarking on the journey of establishing and expanding digital agencies must remain vigilant about emerging technologies, adopt a forward-thinking approach to technology implementation, and prioritize ethical considerations in leveraging technology for business advancement.

Section 1: Chapter 5
Importance of Online Presence

In the digital era, an online presence is the cornerstone of success for businesses of all sizes. For digital agencies, understanding the pivotal role of a strong online presence and guiding clients to establish and maintain it is imperative for sustained growth and visibility in the competitive online landscape.

Foundations of an Effective Online Presence:
Website as a Digital Hub
A website serves as the nucleus of an online presence. It's the first touchpoint for potential clients and a platform to showcase expertise, services, and credibility. An intuitive, responsive, and aesthetically appealing website is paramount for leaving a lasting impression.

Search Engine Optimization (SEO)
Visibility on search engines is critical. Implementing SEO strategies ensures that a website ranks higher in search results, driving organic

traffic and increasing the likelihood of conversions. Optimizing content, meta descriptions, and employing keyword strategies are vital components of effective SEO.

Harnessing the Power of Content:
Content as a Value Proposition
Compelling and relevant content is the lifeblood of an online presence. Blogs, articles, videos, infographics, and other forms of content showcase expertise, provide value to the audience, and establish trust, positioning digital agencies as authorities in their field.

Consistency and Quality
Consistency in delivering high-quality content fosters audience engagement and loyalty. Maintaining a content calendar, addressing trending topics, and ensuring content relevance to the target audience are key to sustaining interest and credibility.

Social Media and Online Branding:
Social Media Platforms
Social media platforms are invaluable tools for enhancing online presence. Each platform offers unique opportunities for engagement, outreach, and brand building. Leveraging platforms like LinkedIn, Twitter, Instagram, and Facebook strategically expands reach and fosters community engagement.

Branding and Storytelling
A cohesive and authentic brand narrative resonates with audiences. Digital agencies must craft a compelling brand story that communicates their mission, values, and unique selling proposition (USP), forging emotional connections with clients and prospects.

Reputation Management and Engagement:
Online Reputation

Monitoring and managing online reputation is critical. Positive reviews, testimonials, and client feedback contribute to a positive brand image. Active engagement and prompt responses to inquiries or feedback demonstrate responsiveness and professionalism.

Interactive Engagement

Encouraging two-way communication with the audience enhances engagement. Conducting webinars, live Q&A sessions, or hosting interactive events humanizes the brand and builds rapport, fostering a sense of community.

Adaptability in a Dynamic Landscape:
Evolving Trends

Adaptability to evolving trends is vital. Staying updated with changing algorithms, emerging platforms, and shifts in consumer behavior ensures relevance and effectiveness in online strategies.

Mobile Optimization

With the proliferation of mobile devices, optimizing online presence for mobile users is non-negotiable. Mobile-friendly websites and content ensure a seamless user experience across devices.

Measurement and Improvement:
Analyzing Metrics

Analyzing performance metrics is integral to enhancing online presence. Key performance indicators (KPIs) such as website traffic, engagement rates, conversion rates, and social media analytics provide insights for refinement.

Iterative Approach

Continuous improvement is a cornerstone of a successful online presence. Iterating strategies based on data-driven insights and feedback ensures ongoing relevance and effectiveness.

Conclusion

In the digital age, a robust online presence is indispensable for digital agencies seeking sustainable growth and visibility. From a compelling website and SEO strategies to engaging content, social media presence, and proactive reputation management, every facet contributes to establishing a strong and credible online footprint.

Understanding the significance of each element and guiding clients to optimize their online presence empowers digital agencies to not only attract and retain clients but also to solidify their position as leaders in the dynamic and competitive online business landscape.

Section 1: Chapter 6
Navigating the Digital Marketing Ecosystem

In the expansive and ever-evolving realm of digital marketing, understanding the multifaceted ecosystem is paramount for online agencies aiming to orchestrate successful campaigns, drive engagement, and deliver tangible results for their clients. This chapter delves into the diverse components of the digital marketing landscape and strategies for effective navigation within it.

Understanding Digital Marketing Components:
Search Engine Marketing (SEM)
SEM encompasses paid strategies to enhance a website's visibility in search engine results. Pay-per-click (PPC) advertising, Google Ads, and sponsored listings are key components that enable agencies to target specific keywords and reach audiences actively searching for related products or services.

Content Marketing

Content is the backbone of digital marketing strategies. Agencies leverage content marketing through blogs, articles, videos, infographics, and eBooks to engage audiences, build brand authority, and foster relationships, ultimately driving conversions.

Email Marketing

Email remains a potent tool for direct communication with audiences. Effective email marketing involves crafting compelling newsletters, personalized messages, and automated campaigns to nurture leads, retain customers, and drive sales.

Social Media Marketing

Social media platforms offer vast opportunities for engagement and brand promotion. Through strategic content, influencer partnerships, community management, and targeted advertising, agencies can reach and engage diverse audiences across platforms.

Influencer Marketing

Collaborating with influencers allows agencies to tap into their followers' trust and influence. Partnering with relevant influencers helps amplify brand messages, reach new audiences, and drive engagement through authentic endorsements.

Crafting Integrated Strategies:
Holistic Approach

Successful digital marketing campaigns often leverage multiple channels and strategies simultaneously. A holistic approach that integrates various components ensures a comprehensive and synergistic marketing effort.

Customer Journey Mapping

Understanding the customer journey is pivotal. Mapping out touchpoints, from initial awareness to conversion and retention, allows agencies to tailor strategies and content that align with customer needs and behaviors at each stage.

Data-Driven Decision Making:
Importance of Data
Data serves as the compass guiding digital marketing strategies. Analyzing metrics, such as click-through rates, conversion rates, engagement metrics, and customer demographics, provides insights for refining strategies and optimizing campaigns.

A/B Testing and Optimization
A/B testing allows agencies to experiment with different variations of content or strategies to determine which yields better results. Continuous optimization based on test outcomes ensures ongoing improvement and efficiency.

Agile and Adaptive Marketing:
Real-Time Adaptation
The digital landscape is dynamic. Agile marketing practices enable agencies to adapt swiftly to emerging trends, capitalize on timely opportunities, and pivot strategies in response to changing consumer behavior or market shifts.

Responsive Campaigns
Developing agile campaigns that respond to real-time events or trending topics can generate rapid engagement and visibility. Being responsive to current affairs or cultural moments can position brands as relevant and relatable.

Compliance and Ethics:

Ethical Considerations

Adherence to ethical practices is essential. Respecting user privacy, ensuring transparency in advertising, and complying with regulations such as GDPR (General Data Protection Regulation) and CCPA (California Consumer Privacy Act) are fundamental.

Brand Authenticity

Maintaining authenticity in marketing efforts builds trust and credibility. Authentic storytelling, genuine engagement, and ethical influencer collaborations contribute to a brand's credibility and long-term relationships with customers.

Conclusion

Navigating the intricate digital marketing ecosystem requires a comprehensive understanding of its diverse components and an agile approach to leverage them effectively. By blending various strategies, leveraging data insights, remaining responsive to trends, and upholding ethical practices, digital agencies can orchestrate impactful and successful marketing campaigns for their clients.

Section 1: Chapter 7
Harnessing the Power of Data and Analytics

In the digital age, data serves as the cornerstone of informed decision-making, strategic planning, and effective execution within online agencies. This chapter explores the significance of data and analytics in guiding crucial business decisions and optimizing performance for digital agencies and their clients.

The Significance of Data in the Digital Landscape:
Data as a Strategic Asset
Data holds immense value as a strategic asset. It provides insights into consumer behavior, market trends, and campaign performance, enabling informed decision-making and the formulation of targeted strategies.

Types of Data

Data comes in various forms: structured, unstructured, quantitative, and qualitative. It encompasses customer demographics, website traffic, engagement metrics, social media interactions, and more, offering a comprehensive view of audience behavior.

Role of Analytics in Business Optimization:
Understanding Analytics

Analytics tools dissect and interpret data, providing actionable insights. They facilitate the extraction of meaningful patterns, trends, and correlations that empower agencies to refine strategies and drive business growth.

Key Performance Indicators (KPIs)

Identifying and monitoring relevant KPIs is pivotal. Metrics like conversion rates, click-through rates, customer acquisition costs, retention rates, and lifetime value guide performance evaluation and optimization.

Implementing Data-Driven Strategies:
Personalization through Data

Data enables personalized experiences. Leveraging customer data allows agencies to tailor marketing messages, product recommendations, and service offerings, enhancing customer satisfaction and driving conversions.

Predictive Analytics

Predictive analytics forecast future trends based on historical data patterns. Agencies can anticipate consumer behavior, market shifts, and campaign outcomes, enabling proactive decision-making and strategy formulation.

Data Collection and Management:

Ethical Data Collection

Ethical data collection practices prioritize user privacy and consent. Agencies must adhere to regulations like GDPR and CCPA, ensuring transparent data collection and usage practices.

Data Quality and Integrity

Maintaining data integrity is crucial. Ensuring data accuracy, consistency, and reliability enhances the credibility of insights derived and informs more reliable decision-making.

Tools and Technologies for Data Analysis:
Analytics Tools

A myriad of analytics tools, such as Google Analytics, Adobe Analytics, and social media analytics platforms, assist agencies in dissecting data and deriving actionable insights tailored to specific marketing channels.

Artificial Intelligence and Machine Learning

AI and machine learning algorithms automate data analysis processes, uncovering complex patterns and correlations at scale, thereby empowering agencies with deeper insights and predictive capabilities.

Data-Driven Decision-Making Process:
Establishing Objectives

Defining clear objectives and key business goals is the foundation. Data analysis should align with these objectives, guiding strategies and initiatives.

Data Interpretation

Interpreting data insights involves extracting meaningful conclusions, recognizing patterns, and identifying actionable takeaways relevant to the business context.

Continuous Optimization and Improvement:
Iterative Approach

An iterative approach to data analysis and strategy optimization is essential. Continuous monitoring, analysis, and refinement ensure adaptability to evolving trends and optimization of performance.

Experimentation and A/B Testing

Experimentation and A/B testing enable agencies to validate hypotheses, refine strategies, and make data-driven decisions, leading to more effective campaigns and business outcomes.

Conclusion

Data and analytics serve as indispensable assets for digital agencies, guiding strategies, and enhancing performance in a competitive landscape. Harnessing the power of data-driven insights enables agencies to optimize marketing efforts, personalize experiences, and drive tangible results for their clients.

Understanding the nuances of data collection, analysis, and ethical usage equips digital agencies with the tools necessary to navigate the complex digital landscape and drive sustained success for themselves and their clients.

Section 1: Chapter 8
Trends Shaping the Future of Online Business

In the ever-evolving landscape of online business, staying abreast of emerging trends and disruptive innovations is pivotal for digital agencies aiming to stay competitive and future-proof their strategies. This chapter explores the transformative trends poised to shape the future of online business, paving the way for new opportunities and challenges.

Rise of Artificial Intelligence (AI) and Automation:
AI-Powered Solutions

Artificial intelligence continues to revolutionize industries. AI-driven automation in customer service, content creation, data analysis, and personalization enhances efficiency, streamlines processes, and enables more targeted and personalized interactions with customers.

Machine Learning Advancements

Advancements in machine learning algorithms enable predictive analytics, enabling businesses to anticipate customer behavior, optimize marketing strategies, and deliver more tailored products and services, thereby enhancing customer satisfaction and driving conversions.

Evolution of Customer Experience (CX):
Hyper-Personalization

Customer experience is becoming increasingly personalized. Businesses leverage data insights to offer highly personalized experiences, tailoring products, recommendations, and marketing messages based on individual preferences and behaviors.

Emphasis on Omnichannel Experience

Seamless omnichannel experiences are imperative. Integrating multiple touchpoints - from websites to mobile apps, social media, and physical stores - creates cohesive and consistent brand experiences, fostering stronger customer relationships.

Growth of E-Commerce and Mobile Commerce:
E-Commerce Expansion

E-commerce continues to expand rapidly. The convergence of online marketplaces, social commerce, and innovative payment solutions amplifies online sales opportunities, providing a broader reach for businesses and streamlining purchasing experiences for consumers.

Mobile-First Approach

The mobile-first approach dominates. As mobile usage surpasses desktop, optimizing websites and experiences for mobile devices becomes paramount, ensuring a smooth and intuitive interface for on-the-go consumers.

Blockchain Technology and Trust:
Enhanced Security and Transparency

Blockchain technology offers enhanced security and transparency. Its decentralized nature enables secure transactions, data verification, and smart contracts, fostering trust among consumers and businesses, particularly in areas like supply chain management and digital contracts.

Impact on Payment Systems

The impact of blockchain extends to payment systems. Cryptocurrencies and blockchain-based payment solutions are disrupting traditional finance, offering faster, more secure, and cost-effective alternatives for online transactions.

Sustainability and Social Responsibility:
Eco-Friendly Practices

Sustainability is gaining prominence. Consumers increasingly prioritize eco-friendly products and ethical business practices, compelling businesses to adopt sustainable production methods, reduce carbon footprints, and embrace corporate social responsibility.

Purpose-Driven Branding

Purpose-driven branding resonates with consumers. Brands that champion social causes, diversity, and inclusivity establish emotional connections with socially conscious consumers, fostering brand loyalty and advocacy.

Augmented Reality (AR) and Virtual Reality (VR):

Immersive Experiences

AR and VR technologies revolutionize experiences. They offer immersive marketing experiences, allowing consumers to interact with products virtually, enhancing engagement and providing more accurate depictions before purchase.

Applications Beyond Entertainment

AR and VR find applications beyond entertainment. Industries such as real estate, healthcare, education, and remote work embrace these technologies for training, simulation, visualization, and remote collaboration.

Data Privacy and Ethical Use of Technology:
Heightened Focus on Privacy

Data privacy remains a focal point. Stricter regulations, consumer awareness, and demands for transparent data practices drive businesses to prioritize data protection and ethical use of customer information.

Ethical AI and Algorithmic Transparency

Ensuring ethical AI and algorithmic transparency is crucial. Businesses must strive for fairness, accountability, and transparency in AI-driven decisions, avoiding bias and ensuring ethical use of automated systems.

Conclusion

The future of online business is a landscape defined by innovation, disruption, and a relentless pursuit of customer-centricity. Leveraging emerging technologies, prioritizing customer experience, sustainability, and ethical practices are essential for digital agencies seeking to thrive in this dynamic environment.

Understanding and embracing these trends provide digital agencies with the foresight and agility needed to adapt, innovate, and capitalize on opportunities, positioning themselves and their clients for success in the ever-evolving online business ecosystem.

Section 1: Chapter 9
Impact of Social Media on Digital Agencies

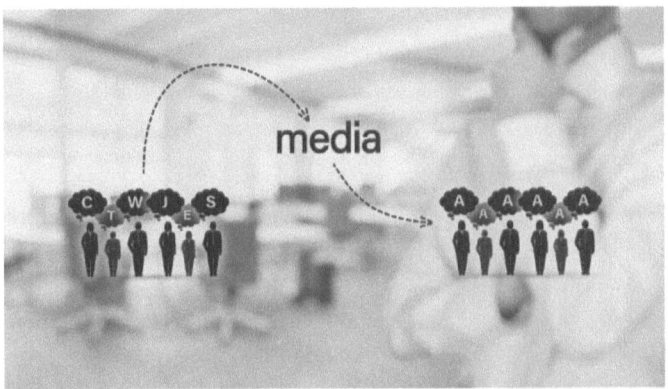

Social media has emerged as a pivotal force in the digital landscape, profoundly impacting how businesses engage with their audiences, market their products or services, and shape their brand presence. This chapter explores the multifaceted impact of social media on digital agencies and their strategies.

Evolution of Social Media in Business:
Shifting Paradigms

Social media has transcended its initial role as a platform for personal interactions. It has evolved into a dynamic ecosystem that facilitates brand-consumer interactions, content dissemination, customer service, and marketing campaigns.

Business-Centric Platforms

Platforms like Facebook, Instagram, Twitter, LinkedIn, TikTok, and YouTube offer diverse opportunities for businesses to connect with their target audiences, share content, and drive engagement through various formats, including posts, stories, videos, and live streams.

Role of Social Media for Digital Agencies:
Amplified Reach and Visibility

Social media offers digital agencies unparalleled reach. Leveraging these platforms, agencies can amplify brand visibility, attract prospects, and engage with a global audience, regardless of geographical constraints.

Engagement and Community Building

Engagement lies at the heart of social media. Digital agencies foster communities around their brands, initiating conversations, responding to queries, and building relationships that cultivate trust and loyalty among followers.

Social Media as a Marketing Tool:
Content Distribution and Promotion

Social media serves as a powerful content distribution channel. Agencies leverage these platforms to disseminate blogs, articles, videos, infographics, and other content formats, driving traffic to websites and enhancing brand exposure.

Targeted Advertising

Sophisticated targeting options in social media advertising enable agencies to reach specific demographics, interests, and behaviors. Customizable ad formats and precise targeting enhance the efficiency and effectiveness of marketing campaigns.

Influencer Partnerships and Collaborations:

Influencer Marketing

Collaborating with influencers allows agencies to tap into their audiences' trust. Influencers endorse products or services, amplifying brand messages and expanding reach, particularly among niche or targeted demographics.

Co-Creation and Partnerships

Digital agencies often engage in co-creation initiatives with influencers or other brands. Collaborative partnerships foster creativity, authenticity, and diversified content, enriching brand narratives and engaging audiences.

Data Insights and Analytics:
Data-Driven Strategies

Social media platforms provide valuable analytics and insights. Agencies utilize these data to refine strategies, measure campaign performance, analyze audience behaviors, and optimize content for better engagement and conversions.

Listening and Feedback

Social listening tools enable agencies to monitor brand mentions, track sentiments, and gather feedback in real-time. This feedback loop aids in understanding customer preferences, addressing concerns, and adapting strategies accordingly.

Challenges and Opportunities:
Content Overload and Attention Economy

The abundance of content poses a challenge. Agencies must curate compelling and relevant content to stand out amidst the content saturation and capture the fleeting attention of their audience.

Real-Time Engagement and Crisis Management

Social media demands immediacy. Agencies need to respond promptly to customer queries, address concerns, and manage crises effectively to maintain brand reputation in real-time.

Ethical Considerations and Transparency: Authenticity and Transparency

Maintaining authenticity is paramount. Agencies must ensure transparency in their social media communications, uphold ethical practices, and avoid misleading or deceptive content to build trust with their audience.

Privacy and Data Security

Respecting user privacy is critical. Agencies must adhere to data protection regulations, secure customer data, and communicate transparently about data collection and usage practices.

Conclusion

Social media has fundamentally transformed how digital agencies operate, market, and engage with their audience. Leveraging these platforms strategically enables agencies to expand their reach, enhance engagement, drive conversions, and build lasting relationships with customers.

Understanding the nuances of social media dynamics, embracing its opportunities, navigating its challenges, and upholding ethical practices empower digital agencies to harness the full potential of these platforms, driving success for themselves and their clients in the digital landscape.

Section 1: Chapter 10
Ethics and Responsibility in the Digital Sphere

In the dynamic and interconnected digital landscape, ethical considerations and social responsibility play a pivotal role in shaping the credibility, trustworthiness, and long-term success of businesses, including digital agencies. This chapter explores the ethical challenges and responsibilities faced by online agencies and strategies to uphold ethical standards in their operations.

Importance of Ethical Practices:
Trust and Credibility

Ethical conduct fosters trust. Upholding ethical standards cultivates credibility, enhancing relationships with clients, stakeholders, and the wider community, which is fundamental for sustained success in the digital realm.

Reputation Management

Maintaining ethical practices safeguards brand reputation. Negative publicity stemming from unethical behavior can have long-term consequences, leading to customer distrust, loss of clients, and damage to the agency's reputation.

Ethical Dilemmas in the Digital Sphere:
Data Privacy and Security

Protecting user data is paramount. Ethical dilemmas arise in data collection, storage, and usage. Agencies must ensure compliance with regulations and prioritize user consent and data security.

Transparency in Advertising and Marketing

Transparency is essential in advertising and marketing. Ethical concerns arise from deceptive practices, false advertising, or undisclosed sponsorships, demanding clear and honest communication with consumers.

Social Responsibility in Online Operations:
Environmental Sustainability

Digital agencies have a role in promoting sustainability. Minimizing environmental impact through eco-friendly practices, reducing carbon footprints, and supporting green initiatives showcase social responsibility.

Diversity, Equity, and Inclusion (DEI)

Promoting diversity and inclusion is vital. Agencies should prioritize creating diverse and inclusive workplaces and advocating for equitable treatment of all individuals, internally and in external engagements.

Challenges in Upholding Ethics:
Rapid Technological Advancements

Technological advancements pose challenges. Agencies must navigate ethical implications of emerging technologies like AI, automation, and data analytics, ensuring responsible and ethical use.

Balancing Profitability and Ethics
Balancing profitability and ethics can be challenging. Agencies may face dilemmas when ethical decisions conflict with financial gains, requiring a delicate balance between profitability and ethical conduct.

Strategies for Ethical Conduct:
Clear Ethical Policies
Establishing clear ethical policies is fundamental. Agencies should articulate and communicate ethical guidelines internally and externally, emphasizing adherence to ethical standards.

Employee Training and Awareness
Educating employees is crucial. Conducting training sessions on ethical practices, promoting awareness, and fostering a culture of ethics empower employees to make ethical decisions.

Transparency and Accountability:
Transparent Communication
Transparent communication builds trust. Agencies should communicate openly about their practices, policies, and operations, maintaining transparency with clients, employees, and stakeholders.

Accountability for Actions
Taking responsibility for actions is essential. Agencies must be accountable for their decisions and actions, addressing mistakes, and rectifying any ethical breaches promptly.

Collaboration and Industry Standards:
Collaborative Efforts

Collaboration within the industry is beneficial. Engaging in industry discussions, sharing best practices, and establishing ethical standards collectively contribute to a more responsible digital sphere.

Adherence to Ethical Guidelines

Agencies should adhere to industry-specific ethical guidelines and standards. Following established codes of conduct and ethical frameworks ensures uniform ethical practices across the industry.

Conclusion

Ethics and social responsibility stand as pillars of credibility and trustworthiness in the digital sphere. Upholding ethical standards is not only a moral obligation but also a strategic imperative for digital agencies, ensuring sustained success and positive contributions to the digital ecosystem.

Navigating ethical challenges, fostering a culture of ethics, maintaining transparency, and collaborating for industry-wide ethical standards empower digital agencies to operate responsibly, building stronger relationships, and making a positive impact in the digital realm.

Section 2: Chapter 1
Ideation: Generating Profitable Business Ideas

The journey of building a successful online agency begins with a compelling and innovative business idea. This chapter explores the art of ideation, offering insights and strategies to foster creativity and generate profitable business ideas for aspiring entrepreneurs in the digital landscape.

Understanding the Ideation Process:
Creativity as a Skill

Creativity is a skill that can be cultivated. It involves generating novel ideas, challenging the status quo, and connecting seemingly unrelated concepts to form innovative solutions.

Problem-Solving Approach

Effective ideation often starts with identifying problems or unmet needs. By understanding pain points, gaps in the market, or areas that need improvement, entrepreneurs can ideate solutions that address these challenges.

Sources of Inspiration:
Market Research and Trends

Conducting thorough market research helps uncover trends, consumer behaviors, and emerging needs. Analyzing market gaps or underserved niches presents opportunities for innovative business ideas.

Consumer Feedback and Insights

Listening to customer feedback provides valuable insights. Understanding customer preferences, pain points, and unfulfilled needs fuels ideation for products or services that cater directly to consumer demands.

Techniques for Idea Generation:
Brainstorming Sessions

Brainstorming fosters idea generation through free-flowing discussions. Encouraging diverse perspectives, setting aside judgment, and allowing ideas to flow freely can lead to innovative concepts.

Mind Mapping and Visualization

Mind mapping visually organizes thoughts and ideas. Mapping out concepts, interlinking ideas, and visualizing relationships can spark new connections and innovative approaches.

Identifying Personal Strengths and Passions:
Leveraging Skills and Expertise

Identifying personal strengths and expertise aids in idea generation. Leveraging existing skills or knowledge in a particular domain can lead to business ideas aligned with one's strengths.

Passion-Driven Ventures

Exploring personal passions often leads to innovative business ideas. Pursuing ventures that align with one's interests fosters motivation and commitment towards building a successful business.

Innovation through Problem-solving:
Identifying Pain Points

Identifying problems or inefficiencies in existing processes or industries presents opportunities for innovative solutions. Solving these pain points can lead to profitable business ideas.

Disruptive Innovation

Disruptive innovation challenges traditional methods or industries. Identifying areas ripe for disruption and offering innovative alternatives can lead to groundbreaking business concepts.

Testing and Validating Ideas:
Prototyping and MVPs

Creating prototypes or Minimum Viable Products (MVPs) helps test ideas. Gathering feedback and iterating based on user responses validate the feasibility and market potential of business ideas.

Market Validation

Conducting market validation tests the viability of business ideas. Surveys, pilot programs, or beta launches gauge market interest and potential demand for the proposed product or service.

Collaborative Ideation:

Networking and Collaboration

Engaging with diverse networks sparks new ideas. Collaborating with experts, mentors, or industry peers fosters idea exchange, feedback, and refinement of business concepts.

Co-Creation and Partnerships

Partnering with others for idea generation fosters innovation. Co-creation initiatives bring together complementary skills and perspectives, leading to unique and robust business ideas.

Embracing Failure and Iteration:
Learning from Failure

Failure is part of the ideation process. Embracing failure as a learning opportunity encourages resilience, adaptation, and refinement of ideas for future success.

Iterative Approach

An iterative approach to ideation involves continuous refinement. Iterating on ideas based on feedback, insights, and changing market dynamics leads to stronger and more viable business concepts.

Conclusion

The process of ideation is the cornerstone of building a successful online agency. Embracing creativity, exploring market needs, leveraging personal strengths, and employing various ideation techniques empower entrepreneurs to generate innovative and profitable business ideas.

Understanding the ideation process, validating ideas, collaborating, and embracing a mindset of continuous improvement and adaptability equips aspiring online agency owners with the foundational elements necessary to kickstart their entrepreneurial journey with robust and promising business concepts.

Section 2: Chapter 2
Market Research and Identifying Opportunities

Effective market research is a cornerstone of success for any online agency. This chapter explores the significance of comprehensive market research and strategies for identifying opportunities in the dynamic and competitive digital landscape.

Importance of Market Research:
Understanding the Landscape
Market research provides a comprehensive view of the competitive landscape. It offers insights into market dynamics, consumer behaviors, industry trends, and competitor strategies, aiding informed decision-making.

Mitigating Risks

Thorough market research minimizes risks. It enables agencies to anticipate challenges, identify potential pitfalls, and devise strategies to mitigate risks associated with entering a specific market or niche.

Components of Market Research:
Industry Analysis

Analyzing the industry landscape reveals market size, growth potential, key players, and industry trends. Understanding industry dynamics guides agencies in identifying lucrative niches or sectors.

Consumer Behavior Insights

Studying consumer behavior is pivotal. Insights into purchasing habits, preferences, pain points, and unmet needs aid in tailoring products or services to meet customer demands effectively.

Techniques for Market Research:
Surveys and Questionnaires

Conducting surveys gathers valuable feedback. Structured questionnaires help gather quantitative and qualitative data, providing insights into consumer preferences and perceptions.

Interviews and Focus Groups

Interviews and focus groups delve deeper into consumer insights. These qualitative research methods uncover nuanced perspectives, motivations, and unexpressed needs of the target audience.

Competitor Analysis:
Identifying Competitors

Analyzing competitors elucidates their strategies, strengths, and weaknesses. Understanding competitor positioning and market share aids in devising differentiated offerings and competitive strategies.

SWOT Analysis
Conducting a SWOT (Strengths, Weaknesses, Opportunities, Threats) analysis helps evaluate market positioning. It aids in identifying unique selling points and potential areas for improvement.

Identifying Opportunities:
Gap Analysis
Gap analysis identifies unmet needs or underserved market segments. Recognizing gaps in existing offerings creates opportunities for agencies to fulfill these needs with innovative solutions.

Trend Identification
Spotting emerging trends is crucial. Staying attuned to technological advancements, shifting consumer behaviors, or industry disruptions presents opportunities for innovative business ideas.

Online Tools and Resources:
Utilizing Analytics Tools
Leveraging analytics tools provides data-driven insights. Platforms like Google Analytics, social media analytics, and market research tools offer valuable data for informed decision-making.

Industry Reports and Publications
Accessing industry reports and publications aids in understanding market trends. Reports from credible sources offer in-depth insights into market forecasts and emerging opportunities.

Emerging Markets and Niches:

Exploring Emerging Markets

Exploring untapped markets or emerging economies presents growth opportunities. Early entry into these markets allows agencies to establish a foothold and gain a competitive edge.

Niche Identification

Identifying specialized niches with specific needs presents opportunities. Focusing on niche markets allows agencies to tailor services/products for a more targeted audience, fostering brand loyalty.

Validating Opportunities:

Pilot Testing and Prototyping

Conducting pilot tests or creating prototypes validates opportunities. Testing product/service ideas with a smaller audience allows for adjustments based on real-world feedback.

Customer Feedback and Iteration

Gathering customer feedback is pivotal. Iterating based on feedback ensures that offerings align with customer needs, preferences, and expectations.

Conclusion

Effective market research and opportunity identification lay the foundation for successful online agencies. By understanding industry dynamics, consumer behavior, competitive landscapes, and emerging trends, agencies can identify lucrative opportunities and tailor their offerings to meet market demands effectively.

Utilizing diverse research methodologies, leveraging online tools and resources, and validating identified opportunities through testing and feedback empower aspiring online agency owners to make informed decisions, capitalize on opportunities, and carve a niche in the competitive digital sphere.

Section 2: Chapter 3
Crafting a Compelling Business
Plan

A well-crafted business plan serves as a roadmap guiding the trajectory of an online agency. This chapter explores the essential components and strategies for creating a comprehensive and compelling business plan that aligns with the goals, vision, and strategies of an aspiring entrepreneur in the digital realm.

Importance of a Business Plan:
Roadmap for Success

A business plan outlines the agency's mission, vision, and strategies. It serves as a roadmap that guides decision-making, goal-setting, and resource allocation for achieving business objectives.

Communication Tool

A well-structured business plan communicates the agency's value proposition, target market, and operational strategies to stakeholders, potential investors, partners, and team members, fostering clarity and alignment.

Key Components of a Business Plan:
Executive Summary
The executive summary encapsulates the essence of the business plan. It provides an overview of the agency, its goals, unique selling proposition (USP), target market, and financial projections.

Company Description
This section details the agency's history, mission, vision, values, legal structure, location, and unique aspects that differentiate it from competitors.

Market Analysis
A comprehensive analysis of the market landscape, including industry trends, target audience demographics, competitor analysis, and identified opportunities, provides insights into market positioning.

Products or Services Offered
Detailing the products or services offered by the agency, their unique features, benefits, pricing strategies, and value propositions helps articulate the agency's offerings.

Marketing and Sales Strategy
Outlining the agency's marketing and sales approaches, including channels, promotional tactics, customer acquisition strategies, and sales projections, aids in envisioning growth.

Operational Plan

The operational plan covers day-to-day operations, organizational structure, staffing, technology requirements, logistics, and supply chain management strategies.

Financial Projections

Financial projections include income statements, cash flow forecasts, balance sheets, break-even analysis, and key financial metrics that provide insights into the agency's financial health and growth potential.

Strategies for Compelling Business Plans:
Clarity and Conciseness

Ensuring clarity and conciseness in language and presentation enhances the business plan's readability. Avoiding jargon and using clear, straightforward language aids comprehension.

Tailoring for the Audience

Adapting the business plan for different audiences is crucial. Investors, partners, or team members may require varying levels of detail and focus, necessitating customization.

Realistic and Achievable Goals

Setting realistic and achievable goals is essential. Providing attainable milestones and timelines ensures credibility and feasibility in the eyes of stakeholders.

Continuous Refinement and Flexibility:
Iterative Approach

Business plans should be iterative documents. Regularly revisiting and updating the plan based on new insights, market changes, and evolving strategies ensures relevance and adaptability.

Flexibility in Execution

Flexibility allows for adaptation to unforeseen circumstances. Business plans should accommodate contingencies and allow for adjustments in strategies based on changing market dynamics.

Use of Visual Aids and Supporting Data:
Visual Representation

Utilizing visual aids like charts, graphs, infographics, and illustrations enhances understanding and engagement. Visual representations simplify complex information and strengthen the plan's impact.

Data and Supporting Evidence

Supporting claims with data and evidence reinforces credibility. Statistics, market research findings, case studies, and testimonials validate assertions made in the business plan.

Conclusion

Crafting a compelling business plan is a fundamental step in establishing a successful online agency. By encapsulating the agency's vision, strategies, market insights, and financial projections in a well-structured document, entrepreneurs can align stakeholders, attract investment, and guide their agency toward achieving its objectives.

Employing strategies such as clarity, tailoring for the audience, continuous refinement, and the use of supporting evidence equips aspiring online agency owners with a powerful tool that not only communicates their vision but also serves as a guiding framework for strategic decision-making and business growth.

Section 2: Chapter 4
Defining Your Unique Selling Proposition (USP)

In a crowded and competitive digital landscape, a Unique Selling Proposition (USP) is the cornerstone of differentiation. This chapter delves into the significance of defining a compelling USP and strategies to craft a distinctive value proposition for an online agency.

Importance of a Unique Selling Proposition:
Setting Your Agency Apart

A USP distinguishes the agency from competitors. It articulates what makes the agency unique, compelling, and preferable to its target audience amidst a sea of options.

Attracting and Retaining Customers

A strong USP resonates with customers. It attracts prospects by addressing their specific needs, fostering interest, and encourages customer loyalty through a clear and memorable value proposition.

Components of a Unique Selling Proposition:
Clear Value Proposition

A USP centers on a clear value proposition. It highlights the primary benefit or solution offered by the agency that resonates with the target audience.

Uniqueness and Differentiation

A compelling USP emphasizes what sets the agency apart. Whether through innovation, specialized services, pricing, customer service, or quality, it showcases a unique advantage.

Strategies for Crafting a USP:
Understanding Target Audience Needs

Understanding the target audience is crucial. Conducting thorough market research aids in identifying pain points, preferences, and unmet needs that the USP can address.

Leveraging Core Competencies

Identifying the agency's core competencies is essential. Leveraging strengths, expertise, or proprietary technologies can form the basis of a strong and differentiated USP.

Clear Communication and Clarity:
Concise and Compelling Messaging

A USP should be communicated concisely. Crafting a succinct and compelling message that encapsulates the agency's unique value resonates more effectively with the audience.

Clarity in Benefits

The USP should clearly articulate the benefits offered. Communicating how the agency's offerings solve problems or fulfill needs ensures clarity and resonates with customers.

Aligning with Brand Identity:
Consistency with Brand Values

The USP should align with the agency's brand values and mission. It should reflect the agency's ethos and promise, reinforcing consistency across all communications.

Integration into Marketing Efforts

Integrating the USP into marketing efforts amplifies its impact. Consistently incorporating the USP across marketing campaigns reinforces brand messaging and differentiation.

Validation and Adaptation:
Customer Feedback and Validation

Gathering feedback validates the USP. Understanding customer perceptions and responses aids in refining and adapting the USP to better align with audience needs.

Adaptability to Market Changes

Adapting the USP to evolving market trends is essential. Flexibility allows the agency to adjust its value proposition to meet changing customer demands and industry dynamics.

Case Studies and Examples:
Real-World Illustrations

Illustrating the USP with case studies or examples reinforces credibility. Sharing success stories or client testimonials validates the agency's unique value proposition.

Competitive Analysis

Comparing the USP with competitors' offerings aids in differentiation. Highlighting where the agency excels compared to others reinforces its unique advantages.

Conclusion

Defining a compelling Unique Selling Proposition is fundamental for an online agency's success. Crafting a USP that effectively communicates the agency's unique value, resonates with the target audience, and differentiates it from competitors is pivotal in gaining market traction and fostering brand loyalty.

Strategies such as understanding audience needs, leveraging core competencies, clarity in communication, alignment with brand identity, continuous validation, and adaptability empower aspiring online agency owners to craft a USP that resonates with customers, sets them apart in the market, and drives business growth.

Section 2: Chapter 5
Creating a Robust Business Model

A well-defined business model serves as the framework upon which a successful online agency is built. This chapter explores the intricacies of creating a robust and adaptable business model tailored to the needs of an online agency in the dynamic digital landscape.

Understanding the Business Model:
Definition and Purpose
A business model outlines how the agency creates, delivers, and captures value. It delineates revenue streams, customer segments, cost structures, and key activities necessary for business operations.

Alignment with Objectives:
A robust business model aligns with the agency's goals and strategies. It supports the vision and mission by providing a roadmap for sustainable growth and profitability.

Key Components of a Business Model:

Value Proposition

The value proposition forms the core of the business model. It outlines the agency's unique value to customers, addressing their needs and differentiating the agency from competitors.

Revenue Streams

Revenue streams detail how the agency generates income. Whether through product sales, subscriptions, service fees, or other monetization strategies, these streams define the agency's financial sustenance.

Customer Segments and Relationships

Identifying customer segments aids in tailoring offerings. Building and nurturing relationships with these segments through effective communication and customer service is pivotal.

Channels and Distribution

Channels represent how the agency reaches customers. Whether through online platforms, direct sales, partnerships, or other distribution methods, these channels facilitate customer interaction.

Key Activities and Resources

Key activities and resources are essential for operations. They encompass core functions, assets, technology, partnerships, and human resources crucial for delivering value.

Cost Structure

The cost structure details expenses incurred. It includes operational costs, infrastructure, marketing expenses, employee salaries, technology investments, and any other costs incurred in running the agency.

Strategies for Creating a Robust Business Model:

Market Validation and Iteration

Validating the business model through market research and iteration ensures viability. Testing assumptions, gathering feedback, and adapting the model based on insights enhance its resilience.

Scalability and Flexibility

Designing the model for scalability allows for growth. Ensuring flexibility enables the model to adapt to market changes, emerging trends, and evolving customer needs.

Innovative Revenue Streams

Identifying diverse revenue streams fosters stability. Exploring innovative monetization strategies beyond traditional models can create additional income sources.

Customer-Centric Approach

Prioritizing a customer-centric model ensures relevance. Tailoring offerings, channels, and relationships around customer needs enhances satisfaction and loyalty.

Technology Integration

Leveraging technology optimizes operations. Integrating tech solutions for efficiency, automation, data analysis, and customer engagement enhances the model's effectiveness.

Risk Management and Contingencies

Addressing risks in the model mitigates potential threats. Anticipating challenges, developing contingencies, and risk management strategies ensure business continuity.

Alignment with Long-Term Goals

Ensuring alignment with long-term objectives fosters sustainability. Aligning the business model with the agency's vision and mission guides decisions for future growth.

Case Studies and Examples

Illustrating successful business models reinforces understanding. Showcasing real-world examples or case studies elucidates effective strategies and implementations.

Continuous Evaluation and Improvement

Regularly evaluating and refining the business model is crucial. Adapting to market dynamics, customer feedback, and changing industry landscapes ensures relevance and competitiveness.

Conclusion

Creating a robust business model is pivotal for the success of an online agency. By comprehensively defining value propositions, revenue streams, customer relationships, operational activities, and cost structures, entrepreneurs can establish a blueprint for sustainable growth and profitability.

Strategies such as market validation, scalability, innovative revenue streams, customer-centricity, technology integration, risk management, alignment with long-term goals, and continuous evaluation empower aspiring online agency owners to craft adaptable, resilient, and successful business models in the ever-evolving digital landscape.

Section 2: Chapter 6
Risk Assessment and Mitigation Strategies

In the dynamic landscape of online agencies, understanding and managing risks are critical for sustained success. This chapter delves into the significance of risk assessment, identification of potential threats, and strategies to mitigate these risks effectively.

Importance of Risk Assessment:
Preparing for Uncertainties
Risk assessment prepares agencies for uncertainties. Identifying potential risks and their impacts aids in devising proactive strategies to mitigate these threats.

Strategic Decision-Making

Understanding risks informs decision-making. Factoring in potential risks enables agencies to make informed choices, minimizing negative consequences and maximizing opportunities.

Identifying Types of Risks:
Market Risks

Market volatility, changing consumer behaviors, and competitive landscape uncertainties pose market risks. Adapting strategies to navigate these fluctuations is essential.

Operational Risks

Operational challenges include technology failures, staffing issues, or process inefficiencies. Streamlining operations and contingency planning mitigate these risks.

Financial Risks

Financial risks involve revenue fluctuations, cash flow issues, or unexpected expenses. Diversifying revenue streams and prudent financial management help manage such risks.

Compliance and Legal Risks

Non-compliance with regulations or legal disputes pose significant threats. Adhering to legal requirements and implementing robust compliance measures mitigate these risks.

Risk Assessment Strategies:
Comprehensive Risk Audit

Conducting a thorough risk audit evaluates potential threats. Identifying, categorizing, and assessing risks quantitatively and qualitatively forms the basis for mitigation plans.

SWOT Analysis

Utilizing SWOT analysis identifies strengths, weaknesses, opportunities, and threats. Understanding internal strengths and vulnerabilities aids in risk mitigation planning.

Scenario Planning:
Anticipating Scenarios
Scenario planning anticipates multiple future scenarios. Preparing strategies for various scenarios helps agencies respond effectively to changing circumstances.

Risk Quantification
Quantifying risks helps prioritize mitigation efforts. Assessing the probability and impact of risks aids in allocating resources for mitigation plans.

Mitigation Strategies:
Contingency Planning
Developing contingency plans prepares for unforeseen events. Establishing alternative courses of action minimizes disruption in case of risks materializing.

Diversification of Resources
Diversifying resources mitigates risks. Spreading resources across different markets, products, or revenue streams minimizes dependency on a single source.

Insurance Coverage
Purchasing insurance coverage hedges against risks. Policies covering liabilities, business interruption, cybersecurity, or other specific risks offer financial protection.

Continuous Monitoring and Adaptation

Regular monitoring aids in risk detection. Adapting strategies based on changing risk landscapes ensures ongoing risk mitigation.

Communication and Training:
Staff Training and Awareness
Educating staff about risks fosters a proactive culture. Training employees to identify risks and respond appropriately strengthens risk management.

Transparent Communication
Open communication channels facilitate risk awareness. Transparent communication about potential risks fosters a shared responsibility for risk mitigation.

Conclusion
Risk assessment and mitigation strategies are integral elements of a successful online agency's operational framework. By comprehensively identifying, assessing, and mitigating potential risks, agencies can navigate uncertainties effectively and ensure business continuity.

Strategies such as conducting comprehensive risk audits, scenario planning, quantification of risks, contingency planning, diversification of resources, insurance coverage, continuous monitoring, staff training, and transparent communication empower aspiring online agency owners to build resilience and adaptability against various threats.

Section 2: Chapter 7
Financial Planning and Budgeting

In the realm of online agencies, prudent financial planning and effective budgeting are pivotal for sustainable growth and success. This chapter explores the significance of financial planning, budget creation, and strategies for sound financial management within the dynamic landscape of digital businesses.

Importance of Financial Planning:
Strategic Decision Making
Financial planning guides strategic decisions. It provides a framework for allocating resources, setting priorities, and planning for business expansion.

Resource Allocation
Effective financial planning ensures optimal resource allocation. It helps in managing cash flow, minimizing costs, and maximizing revenue generation.

Components of Financial Planning:

Revenue Projections

Forecasting revenue helps set realistic targets. Accurate projections aid in planning marketing initiatives, staffing, and operational expansions.

Expense Analysis

Understanding expenses is crucial. Analyzing operational, marketing, and administrative costs aids in identifying areas for cost reduction or optimization.

Cash Flow Management:

Cash Flow Forecasting

Forecasting cash flow ensures liquidity. Monitoring inflows and outflows aids in managing working capital and avoiding cash shortages.

Working Capital Management

Efficient working capital management is essential. Maintaining the right balance ensures the agency can meet short-term financial obligations.

Budget Creation Strategies:

Detailed Expense Budgeting

Creating detailed expense budgets aids in planning. Categorizing and allocating funds for specific purposes helps in cost control.

Revenue Diversification

Diversifying revenue streams stabilizes income. Exploring multiple income sources reduces dependency on a single stream.

Financial Ratios and Metrics:

Key Performance Indicators (KPIs)

Utilizing KPIs measures financial health. Metrics like profit margins, return on investment (ROI), and customer acquisition cost (CAC) provide insights.

Liquidity and Solvency Ratios

Analyzing liquidity and solvency ratios assesses financial stability. Ratios like current ratio and debt-to-equity ratio offer perspectives on financial health.

Risk Management in Finance:

Contingency Funds

Building contingency funds buffers against uncertainties. Reserving funds for unexpected expenses safeguards against financial shocks.

Risk Diversification

Diversifying investments mitigates financial risks. Spreading investments across diverse assets reduces exposure to specific risks.

Financial Planning Tools and Technologies:

Accounting Software

Utilizing accounting software streamlines financial management. Automated tracking, budgeting, and reporting enhance efficiency.

Financial Forecasting Models

Implementing forecasting models aids in projections. Utilizing data-driven models helps in predicting financial outcomes.

Compliance and Regulatory Considerations:

Adhering to Regulations

Complying with financial regulations is imperative. Ensuring adherence to tax laws, accounting standards, and legal obligations is essential.

Financial Audits and Reviews

Conducting financial audits ensures accuracy. Regular reviews reinforce transparency and credibility.

Conclusion

Financial planning and budgeting are fundamental pillars of a successful online agency. By meticulously forecasting revenue, managing expenses, optimizing cash flow, and utilizing financial metrics, agencies can make informed decisions and navigate the competitive digital landscape effectively.

Strategies such as detailed expense budgeting, revenue diversification, financial ratio analysis, risk management, leveraging financial tools, and compliance adherence empower aspiring online agency owners to establish resilient financial frameworks, fostering stability and enabling strategic growth.

Section 2: Chapter 8
Legal Considerations for Digital Agencies

Navigating the legal landscape is essential for the success and sustainability of digital agencies. This chapter explores key legal aspects, compliance requirements, and considerations crucial for operating an online agency within legal frameworks.

Importance of Legal Compliance:
Risk Mitigation
Compliance reduces legal risks. Adhering to laws and regulations mitigates the potential for legal disputes, penalties, and reputational damage.

Credibility and Trust
Operating within legal boundaries builds credibility. Compliance enhances trust among clients, partners, and stakeholders.

Intellectual Property Protection:

Copyrights and Trademarks

Securing copyrights protects original content. Registering trademarks safeguards brand identity and prevents infringement.

Intellectual Property Rights (IPR)

Respecting IPR of others avoids legal issues. Obtaining licenses and permissions for using third-party content ensures legality.

Data Privacy and Security:

Privacy Regulations

Complying with data protection laws is crucial. Safeguarding user data and ensuring compliance with GDPR, CCPA, or other regional privacy regulations is imperative.

Cybersecurity Measures

Implementing robust cybersecurity safeguards data. Encryption, secure networks, and regular audits mitigate cyber threats.

Contractual Agreements:

Client Contracts

Drafting comprehensive client contracts is essential. Clearly outlining services, deliverables, timelines, and payment terms minimizes misunderstandings.

Vendor and Partnership Agreements

Negotiating clear terms with vendors is crucial. Partner agreements specifying responsibilities and expectations avoid conflicts.

Employment and HR Compliance:

Employment Laws

Adhering to employment laws is mandatory. Complying with labor laws, non-discrimination policies, and providing fair working conditions is essential.

HR Policies and Procedures
Implementing HR policies ensures compliance. Addressing hiring practices, employee rights, and disciplinary procedures maintains legal compliance.

Regulatory Compliance:
Industry-Specific Regulations
Understanding industry-specific regulations is necessary. Adhering to sector-specific laws such as finance, healthcare, or advertising regulations is pivotal.

Licensing and Permits
Obtaining necessary licenses is mandatory. Ensuring compliance with local, state, or national licensing requirements is crucial.

Consumer Protection and Liability:
Consumer Rights
Protecting consumer rights is vital. Providing transparent information, honoring warranties, and resolving disputes ethically is crucial.

Liability Insurance
Securing liability insurance mitigates risks. Coverage against potential lawsuits or damages protects the agency's financial health.

Ethical Considerations:
Ethical Marketing Practices

Adhering to ethical standards fosters trust. Avoiding misleading advertising or unethical marketing practices maintains integrity.

Corporate Social Responsibility (CSR)

Embracing CSR initiatives showcases social responsibility. Engaging in philanthropy or sustainable practices contributes positively to society.

Legal Counsel and Advisory:
Seeking Legal Advice

Engaging legal counsel ensures compliance. Consultation for contracts, compliance, or dispute resolution strengthens legal strategies.

Continuous Education and Updates

Staying informed about legal changes is crucial. Continuous learning about evolving laws and regulations is essential for compliance.

Conclusion

Legal considerations form the bedrock of a resilient and trustworthy online agency. By proactively addressing intellectual property protection, data privacy, contractual agreements, employment compliance, regulatory standards, consumer protection, ethics, and seeking legal counsel, agencies can operate within legal frameworks and mitigate risks effectively.

Strategies such as robust contractual agreements, compliance frameworks, ethical practices, liability management, and continuous education empower aspiring online agency owners to navigate the complex legal landscape, fostering credibility, trust, and sustainability within the digital business sphere.

Section 2: Chapter 9
Branding and Positioning
Strategies

In the competitive realm of digital agencies, effective branding and strategic positioning are instrumental for establishing a distinctive identity and resonating with target audiences. This chapter explores the significance of branding, key strategies, and positioning tactics crucial for online agencies to thrive in the digital landscape.

Importance of Branding and Positioning:
Identity and Recognition
Branding defines an agency's identity. It creates recognition and fosters a unique perception among clients, partners, and the industry.

Competitive Differentiation

Strategic positioning sets an agency apart. It defines the unique value and advantages offered compared to competitors, attracting the right audience.

Brand Development Strategies:
Define Brand Identity

Defining brand values, mission, and vision is pivotal. Establishing a brand personality and tone aligns with the agency's ethos.

Visual Branding Elements

Creating visual elements strengthens brand identity. Designing logos, color schemes, typography, and imagery conveys brand consistency.

Brand Messaging and Storytelling:
Crafting Brand Stories

Compelling storytelling resonates with audiences. Narrating brand stories that connect emotionally engages and builds relationships.

Consistent Messaging

Consistency in messaging reinforces brand recall. Aligning communication across platforms maintains brand coherence.

Audience Understanding and Targeting:
Audience Segmentation

Segmenting target audiences aids in tailored strategies. Understanding demographics, behaviors, and needs informs targeted campaigns.

Persona Development

Creating buyer personas enhances targeting. Developing detailed profiles aids in personalized communication and service offerings.

Online Presence and Brand Experience:

Website and User Experience

A well-designed website enhances brand perception. User-friendly interfaces and intuitive navigation provide positive brand experiences.

Social Media Engagement

Active social media engagement boosts brand visibility. Leveraging platforms for communication and community-building strengthens brand presence.

Thought Leadership and Content Strategy:

Thought Leadership Positioning

Establishing expertise elevates the brand. Sharing insights, industry trends, and valuable content positions the agency as a leader.

Content Marketing

Strategic content creation adds value. Producing relevant, informative, and engaging content fosters audience trust.

Collaborations and Partnerships:

Strategic Alliances

Forming partnerships amplifies reach. Collaborating with influencers or complementary brands extends brand exposure.

Industry Participation

Participating in industry events enhances credibility. Speaking engagements, workshops, or conferences elevate brand authority.

Brand Monitoring and Adaptation:

Monitor Brand Perception

Tracking brand sentiment aids in adaptation. Analyzing feedback and adjusting strategies ensures alignment with audience perceptions.

Flexibility and Evolution

Adapting to market changes is essential. Flexibility allows for brand evolution while maintaining core values.

Conclusion

Branding and strategic positioning are fundamental for online agencies seeking recognition and success. By implementing effective brand development strategies, understanding target audiences, ensuring consistent brand experiences, embracing thought leadership, forming collaborations, and continuously monitoring and adapting, agencies can build a strong brand presence in the digital sphere.

Strategies such as defining brand identity, consistent messaging, audience targeting, online experiences, thought leadership, collaborations, and adaptive monitoring empower aspiring online agency owners to craft compelling brands, fostering recognition, trust, and loyalty in the competitive digital market.

Section 2: Chapter 10
Building a Strong Business Foundation

Establishing a solid foundation is crucial for the long-term success and sustainability of an online agency. This chapter explores the essential elements, structural frameworks, and key strategies vital for laying a strong business foundation within the dynamic digital landscape.

Importance of a Strong Business Foundation:
Stability and Resilience

A robust foundation ensures stability. It equips agencies to withstand market fluctuations, challenges, and uncertainties.

Strategic Growth

A strong base facilitates strategic growth. It provides the framework for scalability, innovation, and adaptability in the evolving business environment.

Key Elements of a Business Foundation:
Clear Vision and Mission

Defining a clear vision and mission aligns objectives. It guides decision-making and sets the agency's long-term direction.

Defined Goals and Strategies

Setting specific goals and strategies drives focus. Clear objectives pave the way for systematic execution.

Organizational Structure and Processes:
Efficient Operations

Establishing efficient processes streamlines operations. Structuring workflows, roles, and responsibilities enhances productivity.

Scalable Framework

Designing a scalable structure accommodates growth. Ensuring flexibility allows for easy adaptation to changing needs.

Technology Infrastructure:
Advanced Tools and Systems

Utilizing technology enhances efficiency. Investing in cutting-edge tools supports innovation and streamlines processes.

Cybersecurity Measures

Ensuring robust cybersecurity protects assets. Implementing security protocols safeguards against data breaches.

Financial Health and Management:

Sound Financial Practices

Maintaining financial stability is crucial. Effective budgeting, cash flow management, and risk mitigation strengthen the financial base.

Growth Investment Strategies

Strategically investing in growth initiatives fuels expansion. Allocating resources for innovation and development sustains progress.

Human Resources and Talent Management:
Skilled Workforce

Employing a skilled team drives success. Recruiting, training, and retaining top talent fosters a competitive edge.

Employee Well-being

Prioritizing employee well-being boosts productivity. Creating a conducive work environment supports staff motivation and satisfaction.

Customer-Centric Approach:
Client Relationship Management

Nurturing client relationships builds loyalty. Providing exceptional service enhances customer retention.

Feedback and Improvement

Gathering customer feedback aids in improvement. Listening to client needs ensures service evolution.

Legal Compliance and Ethics:
Adherence to Regulations

Operating within legal boundaries is essential. Ensuring compliance with laws and ethical standards avoids legal issues.

Ethical Practices

Maintaining ethical standards strengthens reputation. Upholding integrity builds trust with stakeholders.

Continuous Improvement and Adaptation:
Iterative Approach

Continuously refining strategies is pivotal. Embracing change and learning from experiences facilitates growth.

Adaptability to Market Dynamics

Adapting to market shifts ensures relevance. Flexibility enables agility in responding to industry changes.

Conclusion

Building a strong business foundation is the bedrock of a successful online agency. By prioritizing elements such as vision and mission alignment, defined strategies, efficient operations, technological advancement, financial stability, talent management, customer-centricity, legal compliance, and adaptability, agencies can establish a resilient framework for sustained growth.

Strategies such as efficient processes, advanced technology integration, sound financial practices, skilled workforce management, client relationship nurturing, ethical practices, and continuous improvement empower aspiring online agency owners to create a robust business foundation, fostering stability, innovation, and competitiveness within the dynamic digital landscape.

Section 3: Chapter 1
Setting Up Your Online Agency Infrastructure

Establishing a robust infrastructure forms the cornerstone of a successful online agency. This chapter explores the foundational elements, technological necessities, and operational structures crucial for setting up an efficient and scalable infrastructure in the digital landscape.

Importance of a Strong Infrastructure:
Operational Efficiency

A well-structured infrastructure streamlines operations. It ensures smooth workflows, reducing bottlenecks and enhancing productivity.

Scalability and Adaptability

A scalable infrastructure accommodates growth. Flexibility allows for seamless adaptation to evolving market needs.

Essential Components of Agency Infrastructure:
Technology and Tools

Utilizing advanced technology is pivotal. Integrated tools for project management, communication, analytics, and automation optimize workflows.

Operational Processes

Establishing streamlined processes is essential. Defined workflows, task assignments, and operational protocols enhance efficiency.

Core Technological Requirements:
Cloud-Based Systems

Utilizing cloud technology offers flexibility. Cloud-based storage, software, and collaborative tools enable remote access and seamless scalability.

Security Measures

Implementing robust cybersecurity is crucial. Firewalls, encryption, multi-factor authentication, and regular audits safeguard against cyber threats.

Project Management Systems:
Efficient Project Tools

Utilizing project management platforms is vital. Tools like Asana, Trello, or Basecamp facilitate task assignments, progress tracking, and collaboration.

Communication Platforms

Effective communication tools enhance productivity. Utilizing platforms like Slack, Microsoft Teams, or Zoom fosters seamless team collaboration.

Customer Relationship Management (CRM):
CRM Integration

Implementing CRM systems streamlines client management. Tools like Salesforce, HubSpot, or Zoho aid in client data organization and engagement.

Automated Marketing Platforms

Utilizing marketing automation tools drives efficiency. Platforms like Mailchimp, Hootsuite, or Buffer automate marketing campaigns and social media management.

Website and Online Presence:
Professional Website Development

Creating a user-friendly website is imperative. A well-designed interface and engaging content enhance brand visibility and customer interaction.

SEO and Content Strategies

Implementing SEO and content plans boosts visibility. Strategic content creation and optimization improve search engine rankings.

Data Analytics and Insights:
Analytical Tools

Utilizing analytics tools aids in decision-making. Platforms like Google Analytics or SEMrush provide insights into user behavior and campaign performance.

Data-Driven Decision Making

Leveraging data guides strategies. Analyzing metrics enables informed adjustments and optimization.

Human Resources and Collaboration:
Talent Management Systems
Implementing HR systems aids in workforce management. Tools like BambooHR or Workday streamline employee data and performance tracking.

Collaboration Software
Facilitating teamwork is essential. Collaboration tools like Google Workspace or Microsoft Office 365 enable seamless teamwork and document sharing.

Continuous Training and Support:
Employee Training Programs
Investing in ongoing training is valuable. Continuous skill development ensures teams are equipped for evolving challenges.

Technical Support and Maintenance
Ensuring continuous support is crucial. Having dedicated technical assistance maintains infrastructure efficiency.

Conclusion
Setting up a robust infrastructure is fundamental for an online agency's success. By integrating technological advancements, establishing efficient processes, leveraging collaborative tools, optimizing online presence, analyzing data insights, nurturing talent, and ensuring continuous support, agencies can create a resilient and scalable infrastructure in the digital realm.

Strategies such as advanced technological integration, streamlined operations, efficient communication, optimized online presence, data-driven decision-making, talent development, and ongoing support empower aspiring online agency owners to establish a strong infrastructure, fostering productivity, innovation, and adaptability in the competitive digital landscape.

Section 3: Chapter 2
Effective Project Management in Digital Agencies

In the dynamic landscape of digital agencies, effective project management is pivotal for delivering quality services, meeting client expectations, and driving operational efficiency. This chapter explores the strategies, methodologies, and tools essential for successful project management within digital agencies.

Importance of Effective Project Management:
Client Satisfaction

Effective project management ensures client satisfaction. Meeting deadlines, delivering quality work, and managing expectations foster positive client relationships.

Operational Efficiency

Streamlined project workflows boost efficiency. Structured processes minimize errors, reduce rework, and optimize resource utilization.

Key Components of Effective Project Management:
Clear Project Objectives
Defining clear project goals is essential. Specific, measurable, achievable, relevant, and time-bound (SMART) objectives guide project direction.

Robust Planning and Scheduling
Thorough planning is crucial. Developing detailed project plans, timelines, and task assignments aids in smooth execution.

Agile Methodology:
Adaptability and Flexibility
Agile methodologies accommodate change. Iterative approaches allow for adjustments based on evolving client needs.

Scrum Framework
Implementing Scrum aids in agility. Sprint planning, daily stand-ups, and retrospectives enhance team collaboration and adaptability.

Waterfall Methodology:
Sequential Approach
The Waterfall model follows a linear sequence. Defined stages ensure clear project phases and deliverables.

Gantt Charts and Milestones
Utilizing Gantt charts tracks progress. Milestones and timelines help in visualizing project stages.

Resource Allocation and Management:
Resource Planning

Optimizing resource allocation is essential. Balancing workloads and skillful task assignments enhance productivity.

Task Prioritization

Prioritizing tasks ensures focus. Identifying critical activities aids in meeting deadlines and managing dependencies.

Communication and Collaboration:
Transparent Communication

Open communication channels foster teamwork. Regular updates, clear instructions, and effective feedback minimize misunderstandings.

Collaboration Tools

Utilizing collaboration platforms enhances coordination. Tools like Slack, Trello, or Microsoft Teams aid in seamless communication.

Risk Management and Problem Solving:
Risk Identification and Mitigation

Proactively addressing risks is crucial. Anticipating potential issues and devising mitigation plans minimizes disruptions.

Problem-Solving Strategies

Effective problem-solving ensures progress. Analyzing challenges and implementing solutions maintains project momentum.

Client Engagement and Feedback:
Continuous Client Interaction

Regular client engagement ensures alignment. Seeking feedback and incorporating suggestions fosters client satisfaction.

Agile Adjustments Based on Feedback

Adapting to client feedback is vital. Iterative changes based on client inputs enhance project deliverables.

Performance Measurement and Evaluation:
Key Performance Indicators (KPIs)

Tracking project performance aids in assessment. Metrics like on-time delivery, client satisfaction, and budget adherence provide insights.

Post-Project Evaluation

Conducting post-project evaluations aids in improvement. Analyzing successes and areas for enhancement guides future projects.

Conclusion

Effective project management is fundamental for the success of digital agencies. By integrating structured methodologies, clear planning, agile adaptation, resource optimization, effective communication, risk management, client engagement, performance evaluation, and continuous improvement, agencies can deliver exceptional results within timelines and budgets.

Strategies such as clear objective setting, methodology alignment, resource optimization, transparent communication, proactive risk management, client collaboration, performance evaluation, and iterative improvements empower aspiring online agency project managers to navigate complexities, ensuring project success and client satisfaction.

Section 3: Chapter 3
Developing a Winning Marketing Strategy

In the highly competitive landscape of digital agencies, a well-crafted marketing strategy is indispensable for attracting clients, building brand awareness, and sustaining business growth. This chapter explores the foundational elements, key tactics, and strategic approaches crucial for formulating an effective marketing strategy within the digital domain.

Importance of a Robust Marketing Strategy:
Brand Visibility and Recognition
A well-defined marketing strategy enhances brand visibility. Consistent messaging and visibility attract potential clients and strengthen brand recognition.

Lead Generation and Conversion

Effective marketing strategies generate leads. Nurturing these leads through strategic tactics converts prospects into paying clients.

Foundational Elements of Marketing Strategy:
Market Analysis and Research

Thorough market analysis informs strategy. Understanding target audiences, competitors, and industry trends aids in developing tailored approaches.

Clear Value Proposition

Articulating a unique value proposition is crucial. Communicating distinct advantages and solutions offered sets the agency apart.

Targeted Marketing Approaches:
Segment-Specific Strategies

Tailoring strategies for different audience segments is effective. Understanding diverse needs allows for personalized approaches.

Content Marketing and SEO

Utilizing content and SEO strategies drives visibility. High-quality content optimized for search engines enhances online presence.

Social Media and Digital Advertising:
Social Media Engagement

Active participation on social platforms boosts engagement. Leveraging platforms for content sharing and interaction enhances brand reach.

Paid Advertising Campaigns

Strategic paid campaigns amplify visibility. Targeted ads on platforms like Google Ads or social media boost lead generation.

Email Marketing and Automation:

Targeted Email Campaigns

Utilizing targeted email campaigns is effective. Personalized messages and automation nurture leads and client relationships.

Marketing Automation Tools

Implementing automation streamlines marketing efforts. Tools like Mailchimp or HubSpot automate tasks and workflows.

Influencer Partnerships and Collaborations:

Influencer Marketing

Collaborating with influencers enhances reach. Partnering with industry-relevant influencers amplifies brand exposure.

Strategic Collaborations

Forming alliances fosters growth. Partnering with complementary brands or agencies expands reach.

Performance Tracking and Analytics:

Analytical Insights

Utilizing analytics informs decision-making. Tracking metrics like conversion rates, engagement, and ROI guides strategy adjustments.

Iterative Improvements

Continuous analysis allows for improvements. Implementing changes based on data insights ensures optimization.

Client Testimonials and Referral Programs:

Client Testimonials and Case Studies

Showcasing client success stories builds credibility. Testimonials and case studies reinforce trust in the agency's capabilities.

Referral Programs

Implementing referral programs encourages advocacy. Incentivizing referrals from satisfied clients expands the client base.

Adaptability and Innovation:
Flexibility in Strategies

Adapting to changing landscapes is essential. Flexibility allows for adjustments based on market shifts and emerging trends.

Innovation and Experimentation

Embracing innovative approaches drives growth. Experimenting with new strategies fosters creativity and differentiation.

Conclusion

A well-crafted marketing strategy is the linchpin of success for digital agencies. By integrating market analysis, value proposition clarity, targeted approaches, content marketing, social media engagement, automation, collaborations, analytics-driven decisions, client testimonials, and adaptive innovation, agencies can create a winning marketing strategy, driving brand visibility, lead generation, and sustained growth.

Strategies such as market analysis, targeted approaches, content marketing, social media engagement, automation, collaborations, analytics-driven decisions, client testimonials, and adaptive innovation empower aspiring online agency owners to navigate the competitive digital landscape, ensuring effective marketing that resonates with target audiences and drives business success.

Section 3: Chapter 4
Client Acquisition and Relationship Management

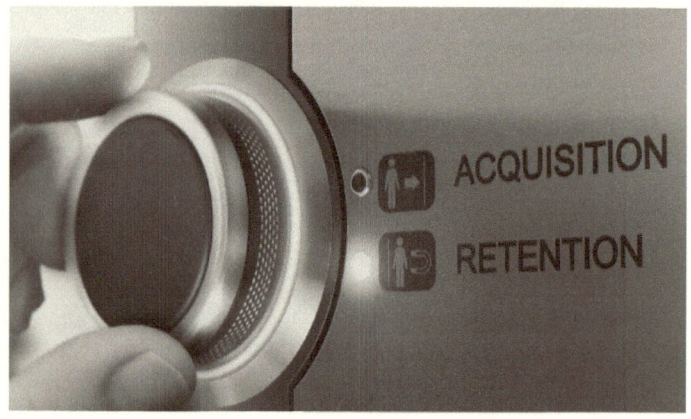

For digital agencies, acquiring clients and maintaining strong relationships are paramount for sustained growth and success. This chapter explores the fundamental strategies, effective tactics, and relationship-building approaches crucial for client acquisition and management within the digital agency sphere.

Importance of Client Acquisition and Relationship Management:
Business Growth and Sustainability

Client acquisition drives business growth. Nurturing client relationships sustains long-term success and repeat business.

Referrals and Reputation

Satisfied clients lead to referrals. Building a positive reputation through strong relationships attracts new clients.

Strategies for Client Acquisition:
Targeted Marketing Campaigns

Strategic marketing efforts attract clients. Tailoring campaigns to specific audiences enhances lead generation.

Networking and Partnerships

Building industry connections is valuable. Networking and forming partnerships expand client reach.

Lead Generation and Conversion:
Effective Lead Generation

Generating quality leads is essential. Leveraging content, SEO, and social media drives lead acquisition.

Conversion Strategies

Nurturing leads into clients is crucial. Effective follow-ups and personalized communication aid in conversion.

Client Onboarding and Engagement:
Seamless Onboarding Processes

Smooth onboarding creates positive experiences. Streamlining processes minimizes friction for new clients.

Continuous Engagement

Maintaining regular communication is vital. Engaging clients through updates and value-driven interactions fosters loyalty.

Client Relationship Management (CRM):
Personalized Communication

Tailoring communication to client needs is crucial. Understanding preferences aids in personalized engagement.

Client Feedback and Satisfaction

Seeking feedback ensures client satisfaction. Addressing concerns and implementing suggestions strengthens relationships.

Retention and Upselling Strategies:
Client Retention Programs

Implementing retention initiatives is valuable. Providing value-added services encourages client loyalty.

Upselling and Cross-Selling

Identifying additional client needs aids in upselling. Offering complementary services enhances value.

Transparency and Trust-Building:
Clear Communication

Transparent communication fosters trust. Providing insights and updates builds credibility.

Delivering on Promises

Meeting commitments strengthens trust. Delivering quality work as promised ensures client satisfaction.

Client Advocacy and Referrals:
Building Client Advocates

Fostering strong relationships creates advocates. Satisfied clients become promoters, aiding in referrals.

Referral Programs

Implementing referral incentives drives advocacy. Encouraging referrals from satisfied clients expands the client base.

Monitoring Client Relationships:
Feedback and Improvement
Regularly seeking feedback aids in improvement. Adapting to client needs ensures ongoing satisfaction.

Analytics and Metrics
Tracking client metrics informs decisions. Analyzing client engagement and satisfaction guides relationship strategies.

Conclusion
Client acquisition and relationship management form the bedrock of success for digital agencies. By integrating targeted marketing, lead generation, client engagement, CRM practices, retention strategies, transparency, trust-building, client advocacy, and continuous monitoring, agencies can acquire new clients and maintain strong relationships, driving business growth and sustainability.

Strategies such as targeted marketing, effective lead conversion, seamless onboarding, personalized engagement, retention initiatives, trust-building, client advocacy, and performance analysis empower aspiring online agency owners to navigate client acquisition and relationship management successfully, ensuring lasting partnerships and business expansion.

Section 3: Chapter 5
Delivering High-Quality Services and Products

For online agencies, delivering exceptional services and products is integral to fostering client satisfaction, building reputation, and ensuring sustained success. This chapter explores the core principles, methodologies, and strategies essential for consistently delivering high-quality services and products in the digital agency landscape.

Importance of High-Quality Deliverables:
Client Satisfaction and Retention
Delivering high-quality work fosters client satisfaction. Exceptional services retain clients and drive referrals.

Reputation and Credibility

Consistency in quality builds reputation. Upholding standards establishes credibility in the industry.

Core Principles of Quality Delivery:
Understanding Client Needs

In-depth comprehension of client requirements is foundational. Aligning services with client objectives is essential.

Clear Expectation Setting

Managing client expectations is crucial. Transparent communication on deliverables and timelines avoids misunderstandings.

Comprehensive Planning and Execution:
Detailed Project Planning

Thorough planning is essential for success. Structuring projects, timelines, and milestones aids in organized execution.

Skilled Execution Teams

Competent teams drive quality. Skilled professionals ensure deliverables meet or exceed expectations.

Continuous Improvement and Innovation:
Iterative Approach

Iterative improvements foster growth. Constantly refining strategies and processes ensures enhancement.

Innovation and Adaptation

Embracing innovation drives quality. Adapting to new technologies and methodologies enables evolution.

Quality Assurance and Testing:

Rigorous Testing Processes

Implementing comprehensive testing is pivotal. QA checks and user testing ensure high-quality deliverables.

Prototyping and Iterative Development

Prototyping aids in quality refinement. Iterative development allows for feedback-driven improvements.

Client Collaboration and Feedback Integration:
Client Participation

Engaging clients in the process enhances quality. Involving them in feedback loops ensures alignment.

Incorporating Feedback

Implementing client suggestions improves deliverables. Adapting based on feedback refines the final output.

Transparency and Communication:
Transparent Reporting

Providing clear progress reports is vital. Transparency ensures clients are informed throughout the process.

Open Communication Channels

Accessible communication fosters trust. Open channels for queries and discussions maintain rapport.

Scalability and Consistency:
Scalable Processes

Scalability ensures consistent quality. Processes adaptable to varying project sizes maintain standards.

Standardized Practices

Upholding consistent quality across projects is crucial. Standardizing practices aids in uniformity.

Post-Delivery Support and Maintenance:
Ongoing Support
Providing post-delivery support builds loyalty. Addressing client concerns post-delivery ensures satisfaction.

Maintenance Services
Offering maintenance ensures long-term value. Supporting products or services post-launch enhances quality perception.

Conclusion
Delivering high-quality services and products is foundational for digital agencies' success. By integrating client understanding, expectation management, comprehensive planning, skilled execution, continuous improvement, quality assurance, client collaboration, transparency, scalability, and post-delivery support, agencies can consistently provide exceptional deliverables, fostering client satisfaction and industry credibility.

Strategies such as detailed planning, skilled execution, continuous improvement, client collaboration, transparency, scalability, and post-delivery support empower aspiring online agency owners to navigate quality delivery successfully, ensuring consistent high standards and client satisfaction.

Section 3: Chapter 6
Optimizing Operations for Efficiency

Efficient operations are the backbone of successful online agencies, enabling streamlined workflows, cost-effectiveness, and improved productivity. This chapter delves into the strategies, methodologies, and best practices crucial for optimizing operations and maximizing efficiency within the dynamic landscape of digital agencies.

Importance of Operational Efficiency:
Productivity Enhancement
Efficient operations drive productivity. Streamlined processes minimize time wastage and maximize output.

Cost Reduction and Resource Optimization
Optimization reduces overheads. Efficient resource allocation ensures cost-effectiveness.

Core Components of Operational Optimization:
Process Analysis and Streamlining
Analyzing and refining processes is essential. Eliminating
redundancies and bottlenecks enhances efficiency.

Workflow Automation
Implementing automation tools boosts productivity. Automated
tasks reduce manual effort and errors.

Technology Integration:
Advanced Tool Utilization
Leveraging technology enhances efficiency. Integrated tools
streamline operations and communication.

Cloud-Based Systems
Adopting cloud technology offers flexibility. Remote access and
scalability optimize operations.

Agile Operations and Adaptability:
Agile Methodologies
Implementing agile frameworks aids in adaptability. Agile
approaches accommodate changes and enhance responsiveness.

Flexibility in Operations
Maintaining flexibility allows for adjustment. Adapting to market
shifts ensures operational relevance.

Resource Allocation and Management:
Resource Optimization
Efficient resource utilization is pivotal. Balancing workloads and
skillful task assignments maximize productivity.

Talent Retention and Development

Investing in talent fosters efficiency. Continuous skill development ensures a competent workforce.

Communication and Collaboration:
Streamlined Communication

Clear communication channels enhance efficiency. Effective communication minimizes errors and delays.

Collaborative Platforms

Utilizing collaboration tools boosts teamwork. Platforms like Slack or Trello aid in seamless coordination.

Project Management Systems:
Efficient Project Tools

Utilizing project management platforms is vital. Tools aid in task assignments and progress tracking.

Agile Project Management

Implementing agile methodologies fosters efficiency. Agile frameworks optimize project workflows.

Continuous Improvement Culture:
Iterative Approach

Continuous refinement drives growth. Regular improvements optimize operations.

Employee Feedback and Involvement

Engaging employees aids in improvement. Encouraging suggestions fosters a culture of improvement.

Data-Driven Decision Making:

Analytical Insights

Utilizing data guides strategies. Analyzing metrics aids in informed decision-making.

Performance Metrics

Tracking performance aids in assessment. Metrics inform adjustments and improvements.

Conclusion

Operational efficiency is fundamental for the success of online agencies. By integrating process analysis, workflow automation, technology utilization, agile methodologies, resource optimization, communication enhancement, project management systems, continuous improvement culture, and data-driven decision-making, agencies can optimize operations for maximal efficiency, driving productivity and cost-effectiveness.

Strategies such as process streamlining, workflow automation, technology integration, agile methodologies, resource optimization, communication enhancement, project management efficiency, continuous improvement culture, and data-driven approaches empower aspiring online agency owners to navigate operational challenges successfully, ensuring streamlined processes and enhanced productivity.

Section 3: Chapter 7
Managing Change and Adapting to Trends

In the ever-evolving landscape of digital agencies, the ability to manage change and adapt to emerging trends is crucial for sustained relevance and success. This chapter explores the strategies, frameworks, and approaches essential for effectively managing change and embracing trends within the dynamic realm of online agencies.

Importance of Managing Change and Embracing Trends: Adaptability and Resilience
The ability to embrace change ensures resilience. Adapting to trends fosters sustainability in a rapidly evolving environment.

Competitive Edge and Innovation

Staying abreast of trends maintains competitiveness. Embracing innovation drives differentiation and growth.

Strategies for Managing Change:
Proactive Approach
Anticipating change is pivotal. Being proactive enables preparedness for evolving circumstances.

Change Management Frameworks
Utilizing structured frameworks aids in change management. Models like Kotter's 8-Step Change Model guide successful transitions.

Embracing Emerging Trends:
Trend Analysis and Prediction
Analyzing trends informs strategy. Understanding emerging technologies and market shifts aids in adaptation.

Innovation and Experimentation
Fostering a culture of innovation is vital. Experimenting with new approaches drives evolution.

Flexibility in Operations and Strategy:
Agile Operations
Maintaining agility ensures adaptability. Agile frameworks enable swift responses to market changes.

Flexible Strategies
Adapting strategies to trends is essential. Flexibility allows for adjustments based on emerging trends.

Talent Development and Reskilling:

Continuous Learning Culture

Encouraging ongoing skill development is crucial. Investing in talent ensures preparedness for change.

Reskilling Initiatives

Adapting skills to meet new demands is vital. Reskilling programs align talent with emerging trends.

Industry Collaboration and Partnerships:
Networking and Alliances

Building industry connections aids in trend identification. Partnerships foster adaptation to market shifts.

Collaborative Innovation

Collaborating with industry players drives innovation. Shared knowledge benefits all stakeholders.

Communication and Change Adoption:
Transparent Communication

Clear communication aids in change adoption. Informing stakeholders fosters alignment.

Change Adoption Strategies

Implementing change gradually aids in adoption. Incremental changes facilitate smoother transitions.

Risk Assessment and Mitigation:
Anticipating Potential Risks

Identifying potential risks ensures preparedness. Risk assessments aid in mitigation planning.

Mitigation Strategies

Planning for contingencies minimizes disruptions. Mitigation strategies reduce the impact of unforeseen events.

Data-Driven Decision Making:
Analyzing Trends and Insights
Utilizing data guides adaptation. Analyzing market insights informs strategic decisions.

Predictive Analytics
Forecasting trends aids in preparedness. Predictive analytics assist in anticipating future changes.

Conclusion
Managing change and embracing trends are pivotal for the sustainability of online agencies. By integrating proactive change management, trend analysis, innovation, flexibility, talent development, industry collaborations, communication strategies, risk mitigation, and data-driven decision-making, agencies can effectively navigate change, ensuring adaptability and sustained relevance in the competitive digital landscape.

Strategies such as proactive change management, trend analysis, innovation, flexibility, talent development, collaborations, communication strategies, risk mitigation, and data-driven approaches empower aspiring online agency owners to successfully manage change and embrace trends, fostering resilience and competitiveness in the dynamic digital sphere.

Section 3: Chapter 8
Overcoming Common Challenges
in Execution

Execution is the bridge between ideas and results, yet numerous challenges can impede the smooth realization of plans within online agencies. This chapter delves into identifying, addressing, and overcoming common challenges encountered during execution in the digital agency landscape.

Understanding Execution Challenges:
Scope Creep and Shifting Priorities
Uncontrolled expansion of project scope disrupts execution. Shifting priorities hinder progress and focus.

Resource Constraints and Allocation
Limited resources pose challenges. Inadequate resource allocation impacts project timelines and quality.

Common Challenges Faced in Execution:
Poor Project Planning
Incomplete or inadequate planning hampers execution.
Insufficiently scoped projects lead to delays and overspending.

Communication Gaps
Ineffective communication impedes progress. Misunderstandings or
lack of clarity disrupt workflows.

Strategies for Overcoming Execution Challenges:
Robust Project Planning
Thorough planning mitigates challenges. Detailed project scopes
and timelines ensure clarity.

Agile Methodologies
Adopting agile frameworks aids in adaptability. Iterative
approaches accommodate evolving requirements.

Efficient Resource Allocation
Optimizing resource distribution is pivotal. Balancing workloads
and skillful task assignments enhances productivity.

Enhanced Communication Channels
Effective communication minimizes errors. Transparent and
accessible channels foster collaboration.

Managing Scope Creep and Priorities:
Scope Management Strategies
Implementing scope controls prevents creep. Clear requirements
and change control processes aid in managing scope.

Prioritization Techniques

Setting clear priorities aids in focus. Ranking tasks based on urgency ensures efficient execution.

Addressing Resource Constraints:
Resource Optimization
Optimizing resource utilization is crucial. Efficiently allocating resources maximizes productivity.

Outsourcing and Partnerships
Collaborating with external partners aids in resource augmentation. Outsourcing specialized tasks mitigates constraints.

Collaborative Project Management:
Project Management Tools
Utilizing robust project management platforms aids in coordination. Tools like Asana or Jira streamline workflows.

Cross-Functional Teams
Building diverse teams ensures adaptability. Multifunctional teams offer varied expertise for complex projects.

Risk Mitigation Strategies:
Risk Identification
Anticipating potential risks is crucial. Identifying risks allows for proactive mitigation planning.

Contingency Planning
Developing contingency plans minimizes disruptions. Preparing for unforeseen events reduces their impact.

Monitoring and Adaptation:
Continuous Monitoring

Regularly tracking progress is vital. Timely identification of issues enables swift corrective actions.

Adaptive Approaches

Adapting to changes ensures flexibility. Swift adjustments based on monitoring prevent setbacks.

Conclusion

Execution challenges are inherent in the journey of online agencies. By integrating robust planning, agile methodologies, resource optimization, enhanced communication, scope management, prioritization, addressing resource constraints, collaborative project management, risk mitigation, monitoring, and adaptive approaches, agencies can navigate and overcome common execution challenges, ensuring smoother project execution and success.

Strategies such as robust planning, agile methodologies, resource optimization, communication enhancement, scope management, prioritization, addressing constraints, collaborative project management, risk mitigation, monitoring, and adaptive approaches empower aspiring online agency owners to overcome execution challenges, fostering efficiency and achieving project goals.

Section 3: Chapter 9
Agility and Innovation in Digital Agency Practices

In the dynamic realm of digital agencies, agility and innovation are linchpins for sustained growth and competitiveness. This chapter delves into the significance of agility and innovation, exploring strategies, methodologies, and best practices crucial for fostering an agile and innovative culture within online agencies.

Importance of Agility and Innovation:
Adaptability to Change
Agility ensures adaptability. Embracing innovation drives evolution amid market shifts.

Competitive Edge and Differentiation
Staying agile fosters competitiveness. Innovation drives differentiation and enhances value propositions.

Embracing Agile Methodologies:
Agile Frameworks
Adopting agile methodologies aids in adaptability. Scrum, Kanban, or Lean practices enable responsiveness.

Iterative Approaches
Implementing iterative processes fosters agility. Incremental improvements ensure flexibility.

Cultivating an Innovative Culture:
Promoting Creativity
Encouraging creative thinking drives innovation. Openness to new ideas fosters a culture of innovation.

Experimentation and Risk-Taking
Embracing experimentation allows for breakthroughs. Encouraging calculated risk-taking drives innovation.

Strategies for Agility and Innovation:
Cross-Functional Collaboration
Fostering collaboration among diverse teams aids in innovation. Varied perspectives drive creative solutions.

Rapid Prototyping
Implementing rapid prototyping aids in innovation. Quick iterations allow for testing and feedback.

Client-Centric Approaches:
Co-Creation with Clients
Involving clients in the innovation process enhances solutions. Collaborating on ideas ensures relevance.

Client Feedback Integration

Incorporating client feedback drives innovation. Adapting based on input ensures client satisfaction.

Technology Integration for Innovation:
Leveraging Emerging Technologies

Utilizing new tech drives innovation. AI, AR/VR, or blockchain integration fosters creative solutions.

Digital Transformation Initiatives

Implementing digital transformation enhances agility. Automating processes drives efficiency and innovation.

Continuous Learning and Development
Upskilling Initiatives

Investing in talent drives innovation. Continuous skill development ensures adaptability to new trends.

Innovation Workshops and Training

Conducting innovation workshops fosters creativity. Training sessions drive ideation and problem-solving skills.

Adaptability to Market Shifts:
Market Analysis and Trend Monitoring

Constantly monitoring trends aids in agility. Adapting to market shifts ensures relevance.

Flexible Strategies

Maintaining flexibility allows for adaptation. Adjusting strategies based on emerging trends fosters agility.

Risk-Taking and Adaptation:

Encouraging Risk-Taking

Promoting calculated risks drives innovation. Encouraging experimentation allows for breakthroughs.

Adaptive Approaches

Adapting to changes ensures flexibility. Swift adjustments based on market shifts prevent stagnation.

Conclusion

Agility and innovation form the bedrock of success for digital agencies. By integrating agile methodologies, innovative cultures, cross-functional collaboration, client-centric approaches, technology integration, continuous learning, adaptability, and risk-taking, agencies can foster agility and innovation, driving evolution and competitiveness in the dynamic digital landscape.

Strategies such as agile methodologies, innovative cultures, client-centric approaches, technology integration, continuous learning, adaptability, and risk-taking empower aspiring online agency owners to foster agility and innovation, nurturing a culture that embraces change and drives creative solutions.

.

Section 3: Chapter 10
Continuous Improvement and Growth

In the competitive landscape of digital agencies, continuous improvement is indispensable for sustained growth and staying ahead. This chapter explores the significance of continuous improvement, strategies, methodologies, and best practices crucial for fostering a culture of growth within online agencies.

Importance of Continuous Improvement:
Evolution and Adaptation
Continuous improvement drives evolution. Adaptation to new trends ensures relevance.

Competitive Advantage
Consistent growth fosters competitiveness. Incremental improvements lead to substantial advantages.

Cultivating a Culture of Improvement:
Embracing Kaizen Principles

Adopting Kaizen fosters continuous improvement. Small, incremental changes drive long-term growth.

Learning from Failures

Viewing failures as learning opportunities aids improvement. Analyzing missteps drives better outcomes.

Strategies for Continuous Improvement:
Lean Methodologies

Implementing lean practices streamlines processes. Eliminating waste drives efficiency and growth.

Six Sigma Principles

Utilizing Six Sigma enhances quality. Data-driven approaches ensure consistent improvement.

Data-Driven Decision Making:
Utilizing Analytics

Leveraging data guides improvements. Analyzing metrics aids in informed decision-making.

Performance Metrics

Tracking performance aids in assessment. Metrics inform adjustments and improvements.

Feedback and Adaptation:
Stakeholder Feedback

Seeking feedback ensures continuous improvement. Addressing concerns drives better outcomes.

Adaptive Approaches

Adapting to feedback ensures growth. Implementing changes fosters evolution.

Innovation and Experimentation:
Encouraging Creativity

Fostering a culture of innovation drives growth. Openness to new ideas spurs evolution.

Experimentation with New Ideas

Implementing experimental initiatives aids growth. Trying new approaches drives innovation.

Process Optimization:
Streamlining Workflows

Continuous refinement drives efficiency. Eliminating bottlenecks ensures smoother operations.

Automation and Technology Integration

Leveraging technology aids in growth. Automating processes enhances productivity.

Talent Development and Empowerment:
Continuous Learning Initiatives

Investing in talent drives growth. Continuous skill development ensures adaptability.

Empowering Employees

Encouraging autonomy fosters growth. Empowered teams drive innovative solutions.

Market Analysis and Adaptability:

Trend Monitoring

Constantly monitoring trends aids in growth. Adapting to market shifts ensures relevance.

Flexible Strategies

Maintaining flexibility allows for adaptation. Adjusting strategies based on emerging trends drives growth.

Conclusion

Continuous improvement is fundamental for the success of digital agencies. By integrating Kaizen principles, lean methodologies, data-driven decision-making, feedback incorporation, innovation, process optimization, talent development, adaptability, and market analysis, agencies can foster a culture of continuous improvement, driving growth and staying competitive in the ever-evolving digital landscape.

Strategies such as lean methodologies, data-driven decision-making, feedback incorporation, innovation, process optimization, talent development, adaptability, and market analysis empower aspiring online agency owners to cultivate continuous improvement, nurturing a culture that drives consistent growth and ensures sustained success.

Section 4: Chapter 1
Recruitment Strategies for Digital Agencies

Recruiting top talent is pivotal for the success and growth of digital agencies. This chapter delves into effective recruitment strategies, methodologies, and best practices tailored to the dynamic needs of online agencies.

Importance of Effective Recruitment:
Talent as an Asset
Skilled professionals drive agency success. Recruiting top talent is essential for growth.

Competitive Edge
Attracting the right talent fosters competitiveness. Skilled teams differentiate agencies in the market.

Tailored Recruitment Strategies:
Define Job Roles Clearly

Clearly defined job roles attract suitable candidates. Detailed descriptions ensure alignment of expectations.

Targeted Talent Search

Strategic talent sourcing is crucial. Targeting platforms or networks relevant to the industry aids in finding niche talent.

Employer Branding and Positioning:
Building a Strong Brand Image

A positive brand image attracts talent. Showcasing agency culture and success stories enhances attractiveness.

Positioning as an Employer of Choice

Emphasizing employee benefits and career growth opportunities positions the agency attractively.

Innovative Recruitment Approaches:
Utilizing Social Media Platforms

Leveraging social networks aids in talent discovery. Engaging content showcases the agency's culture and values.

Employee Referral Programs

Encouraging referrals from existing employees is valuable. Trusting connections aid in recruiting suitable candidates.

Streamlined Recruitment Processes:
Efficient Screening and Selection

Streamlining the screening process saves time. Efficient selection methodologies identify the best candidates.

Personalized Interviews

Tailoring interviews to roles aids in assessment. Personalized interviews assess candidates effectively.

Agile Talent Management:
Flexible Work Structures

Offering flexible work arrangements attracts talent. Remote work options and flexible hours appeal to a diverse talent pool.

Continuous Talent Development

Investing in employee growth ensures retention. Continuous learning opportunities foster loyalty.

Diversity and Inclusion Initiatives:
Promoting Diversity

Diverse teams drive innovation. Inclusive recruitment practices enhance creativity and problem-solving.

Eliminating Bias in Recruitment

Removing biases ensures fair selection. Implementing blind hiring practices aids in unbiased recruitment.

Collaboration with Educational Institutions:
Internship and Graduate Programs

Engaging with educational institutions aids in talent acquisition. Internship programs often lead to full-time hires.

Training Partnerships

Collaborating with educational bodies ensures skilled graduates. Tailored programs meet agency-specific needs.

Metrics and Analysis:

Recruitment Analytics

Tracking recruitment metrics aids in assessment. Analyzing success rates refines future recruitment strategies.

Feedback Integration

Incorporating candidate and employee feedback ensures improvement. Identifying areas for enhancement refines recruitment processes.

Conclusion

Effective recruitment strategies are the cornerstone of digital agency success. By integrating tailored recruitment approaches, employer branding, innovative strategies, streamlined processes, agile talent management, diversity initiatives, educational collaborations, and data-driven analytics, agencies can attract and retain top talent, driving growth and competitiveness in the evolving digital landscape.

Strategies such as clear job role definitions, targeted talent searches, employer branding, innovative recruitment approaches, streamlined processes, agile talent management, diversity initiatives, educational collaborations, and recruitment analytics empower aspiring online agency owners to build and retain high-performing teams, ensuring sustained success and growth.

Section 4: Chapter 2
Cultivating a Positive Company Culture

A robust company culture is the cornerstone of a thriving digital agency. This chapter explores the significance of fostering a positive company culture, strategies, methodologies, and best practices essential for cultivating a dynamic and engaging work environment within online agencies.

Importance of a Positive Company Culture:
Employee Engagement and Retention
A positive culture fosters engagement. Satisfied employees are more likely to stay and contribute positively.

Enhanced Productivity and Innovation
A supportive environment drives productivity. Open cultures encourage innovative thinking and problem-solving.

Defining Company Values and Vision:
Establishing Core Values

Defining core values guides behavior. Shared values align
employees and drive a unified culture.

Vision Communication

Communicating a compelling vision inspires. Sharing the agency's
goals motivates employees.

Fostering an Inclusive Environment:
Embracing Diversity

Diverse cultures drive innovation. Inclusive practices create a sense
of belonging.

Open Communication Channels

Encouraging dialogue fosters inclusion. Transparent communication
ensures everyone's voices are heard.

Employee Well-being Initiatives
Work-Life Balance Advocacy

Promoting work-life balance enhances well-being. Flexible work
arrangements support employee needs.

Mental Health Support

Supporting mental health is crucial. Wellness programs and
resources aid in mental well-being.

Encouraging Collaboration and Teamwork
Team-building Activities

Engaging team events foster relationships. Collaboration is
encouraged through shared experiences.

Cross-functional Projects

Assigning cross-departmental tasks drives collaboration. Diverse skill sets work together for common goals.

Recognition and Appreciation:
Acknowledging Achievements

Celebrating successes boosts morale. Recognizing accomplishments motivates employees.

Feedback and Development

Constructive feedback aids growth. Encouraging continuous improvement enhances employee development.

Leadership and Role Modeling:
Lead by Example

Leaders shaping culture through actions. Displaying desired behaviors influences the team.

Empowerment and Trust

Empowering employees fosters autonomy. Trusting teams encourages responsibility and innovation.

Learning and Development Culture:
Continuous Learning Initiatives

Investing in skill development aids growth. Learning opportunities enhance employee engagement.

Knowledge Sharing

Encouraging knowledge exchange drives innovation. Cross-pollination of ideas fosters creativity.

Cultural Assessments and Adaptations:

Cultural Surveys

Gauging employee satisfaction aids in assessment. Surveys inform areas for cultural improvements.

Adaptation to Change

Adapting culture to evolving needs is crucial. Flexibility ensures relevance and employee satisfaction.

Conclusion

A positive company culture is fundamental for the success and growth of digital agencies. By integrating core values, inclusive environments, employee well-being initiatives, collaboration promotion, recognition practices, leadership role modeling, learning cultures, and cultural assessments, agencies can cultivate a positive and engaging work environment, driving employee satisfaction, productivity, and innovation.

Strategies such as defining values, fostering inclusivity, promoting well-being, encouraging collaboration, recognizing achievements, empowering leadership, learning cultures, and cultural assessments empower aspiring online agency owners to build a dynamic and positive company culture, ensuring a motivated and engaged workforce, and sustained success.

Section 4: Chapter 3
Leadership and Team Management

Effective leadership and proficient team management are crucial pillars for the success and growth of digital agencies. This chapter explores the significance of strong leadership, strategies, methodologies, and best practices essential for effective leadership and team management within online agencies.

Importance of Effective Leadership:
Visionary Guidance
Leaders provide direction. A clear vision motivates and aligns teams towards common goals.

Inspirational Role Modeling
Leaders set examples. Role modeling desired behaviors influences team culture.

Defining Leadership Styles:

Adaptive Leadership

Adapting leadership styles to situations aids effectiveness. Flexibility ensures alignment with team needs.

Servant Leadership

Fostering a servant leadership approach aids teamwork. Prioritizing team needs drives collective success.

Communication and Transparency:
Open Communication

Transparent dialogue builds trust. Clear communication fosters team cohesion and understanding.

Active Listening

Listening fosters connection. Understanding team concerns aids in effective decision-making.

Empowerment and Delegation:
Empowering Teams

Empowerment drives motivation. Trusting teams encourages ownership and innovation.

Delegation Strategies

Effective delegation aids in efficiency. Delegating tasks based on team strengths ensures success.

Conflict Resolution and Mediation:
Conflict Management Skills

Addressing conflicts ensures harmony. Mediation and conflict resolution skills mitigate disruptions.

Constructive Feedback

Providing constructive feedback aids growth. Addressing issues ensures continuous improvement.

Team Building and Motivation:
Building Strong Teams
Fostering team cohesion drives productivity. Team-building activities enhance collaboration.

Motivational Strategies
Recognizing achievements boosts morale. Motivated teams drive impactful results.

Goal Setting and Accountability:
Setting Clear Objectives
Defining goals guides actions. Clear objectives align efforts toward achieving results.

Accountability Measures
Accountability drives responsibility. Tracking progress ensures goal attainment.

Coaching and Development:
Mentorship and Guidance
Offering mentorship aids growth. Guidance from experienced leaders enhances skills.

Continuous Learning Culture
Encouraging ongoing skill development ensures adaptability. Learning opportunities foster engagement.

Adaptability and Change Management:
Adapting to Market Shifts

Flexible leadership ensures adaptability. Adapting strategies to market changes fosters relevance.

Change Management Skills

Effective change management aids transitions. Navigating changes ensures team stability.

Conclusion

Effective leadership and proficient team management are pivotal for the success of digital agencies. By integrating visionary guidance, adaptive leadership, transparent communication, empowerment, conflict resolution, team building, goal setting, coaching, adaptability, and change management, agencies can cultivate strong leadership and proficient team management, fostering a motivated, engaged, and high-performing workforce.

Strategies such as adaptive leadership, effective communication, empowerment, conflict resolution, team building, goal setting, coaching, adaptability, and change management empower aspiring online agency owners to lead effectively, manage teams proficiently, and drive sustained success and growth.

Section 4: Chapter 4
Training and Skill Development

Continuous training and skill development are vital components for the growth and competitiveness of digital agencies. This chapter explores the significance of training, strategies, methodologies, and best practices essential for fostering a culture of continuous learning and skill development within online agencies.

Importance of Training and Skill Development:
Adaptability to Changes
Ongoing training ensures adaptability. Updated skills align employees with industry advancements.

Enhanced Performance and Innovation
Continuous learning drives performance. Enhanced skills foster innovative solutions and creativity.

Identifying Training Needs:

Skills Gap Analysis

Assessing skills aids in identifying gaps. Understanding training needs ensures targeted development.

Future Skills Projections

Predicting industry trends guides training. Preparing for future demands ensures preparedness.

Implementing Effective Training Programs:
Tailored Learning Paths

Customized training meets specific needs. Tailoring programs to roles ensures relevance.

Diverse Training Formats

Utilizing varied formats aids learning. Workshops, e-learning, and mentorship drive diverse skill acquisition.

Technology and Tools Training:
Emerging Tech Integration

Training on new technologies aids adaptation. Upskilling on AI, automation, etc., ensures proficiency.

Software and Tools Mastery

Mastery of industry tools enhances efficiency. Proficiency drives productivity and quality.

Soft Skills Development:
Communication and Collaboration

Enhancing interpersonal skills aids teamwork. Effective communication fosters collaboration.

Leadership and Management

Developing leadership skills aids growth. Training on management drives effective team management.

Learning Platforms and Resources:
Online Learning Platforms

Utilizing e-learning aids accessibility. Platforms like Coursera or LinkedIn Learning offer diverse courses.

In-house Training Resources

Developing in-house materials aids training. Customized resources align with agency needs.

Mentorship and Coaching:
Senior-Level Guidance

Mentorship drives professional growth. Guidance from experienced leaders aids skill enhancement.

Coaching Initiatives

Offering coaching programs enhances skills. Structured coaching aids in skill development.

Continuous Learning Culture:
Encouraging Curiosity

Fostering a thirst for learning aids development. Curiosity drives exploration of new skills.

Rewarding Learning

Recognizing learning achievements motivates. Incentivizing training fosters a learning culture.

Evaluation and Feedback:
Training Impact Assessment

Assessing training effectiveness aids improvement. Metrics guide future training plans.

Feedback Integration

Incorporating learner feedback refines programs. Addressing concerns ensures quality training.

Conclusion

Continuous training and skill development are essential for the growth and sustainability of digital agencies. By integrating skills gap analysis, tailored programs, technology training, soft skills development, learning platforms, mentorship, coaching, continuous learning cultures, and evaluation processes, agencies can foster a culture of continuous learning and skill enhancement, driving employee competence and agency competitiveness.

Strategies such as skills gap analysis, tailored training programs, technology and tools training, soft skills development, learning platforms, mentorship, coaching, continuous learning cultures, and evaluation processes empower aspiring online agency owners to invest in training, ensuring a skilled workforce, sustained growth, and adaptability to industry changes.

Section 4: Chapter 5
Remote Work and Virtual Teams

The rise of remote work has transformed the landscape of digital agencies. This chapter explores the significance of remote work, strategies, methodologies, and best practices essential for managing remote teams and fostering a successful virtual work environment within online agencies.

Importance of Remote Work:
Flexibility and Access to Talent
Remote work expands talent pools. Access to global talent drives diversity and expertise.

Work-Life Balance and Productivity
Flexible work arrangements enhance well-being. Enhanced flexibility boosts productivity and job satisfaction.

Building a Remote Work Culture:
Clear Remote Work Policies

Defining remote work guidelines aids clarity. Policies ensure consistency across remote teams.

Trust and Communication

Building trust drives remote team success. Transparent communication fosters team cohesion.

Effective Remote Team Management:
Structured Communication Channels

Utilizing communication tools aids collaboration. Platforms like Slack or Zoom streamline interactions.

Regular Check-Ins

Frequent meetings ensure alignment. Regular updates enhance accountability and progress tracking.

Setting Clear Goals and Expectations:
Defined Objectives

Clear goals guide remote work. Specific objectives ensure focus and clarity.

Performance Metrics

Tracking progress aids evaluation. Metrics drive accountability and goal achievement.

Collaboration and Engagement:
Team Collaboration Tools

Utilizing collaborative platforms aids teamwork. Tools like Trello or Google Workspace enhance collaboration.

Virtual Team-building Activities

Engaging team events foster relationships. Virtual activities boost team morale and connectivity.

Ensuring Work Efficiency:
Time Management Strategies

Efficient time management enhances productivity. Setting schedules aids in task prioritization.

Flexible Work Arrangements

Adapting to diverse time zones aids flexibility. Accommodating schedules ensures productivity.

Cybersecurity and Remote Work:
Secure Data Handling

Ensuring data protection is vital. Cybersecurity protocols safeguard sensitive information.

Training on Security Measures

Educating employees on security practices mitigates risks. Awareness prevents potential breaches.

Remote Work Challenges and Solutions:
Overcoming Communication Barriers

Effective communication resolves misunderstandings. Clear directives avoid confusion.

Combatting Isolation

Fostering a sense of belonging aids remote team morale. Regular interactions boost team spirit.

Cultivating Company Culture Remotely:

Virtual Culture Initiatives

Virtual events maintain culture. Celebrating milestones virtually fosters team spirit.

Inclusive Practices

Including remote employees in office events aids inclusion. Equal participation enhances connectivity.

Conclusion

Remote work has become integral to the operations of digital agencies. By integrating clear policies, effective communication, goal setting, collaboration tools, efficient work strategies, cybersecurity measures, addressing challenges, and nurturing remote company culture, agencies can successfully manage remote teams, driving productivity, connectivity, and growth.

Strategies such as clear remote work policies, effective communication, goal setting, collaboration tools, efficient work strategies, cybersecurity measures, addressing challenges, and nurturing remote company culture empower aspiring online agency owners to effectively manage remote teams, ensuring productivity and success in the evolving landscape.

Section 4: Chapter 6
Fostering Collaboration and Creativity

Collaboration and creativity are fundamental elements in driving innovation within digital agencies. This chapter explores the significance of fostering collaboration and nurturing creativity, strategies, methodologies, and best practices essential for cultivating a dynamic and innovative environment within online agencies.

Importance of Collaboration and Creativity:
Innovative Solutions
Collaboration sparks diverse ideas. Creativity drives innovative problem-solving.

Enhanced Team Engagement

Collaborative environments foster engagement. Creative outlets boost employee satisfaction.

Creating Collaborative Workspaces:
Virtual Collaboration Tools
Utilizing digital platforms aids teamwork. Tools like Microsoft Teams or Asana enhance collaboration.

Physical Collaboration Spaces
Designating areas for teamwork fosters creativity. Office spaces encourage face-to-face interactions.

Cross-Functional Collaboration:
Breaking Silos
Encouraging interactions between departments drives innovation. Diverse perspectives fuel creative solutions.

Interdisciplinary Projects
Assigning projects involving multiple skill sets fosters collaboration. Cross-pollination drives creativity.

Effective Brainstorming Sessions:
Structured Brainstorming
Guided sessions enhance idea generation. Structured approaches ensure fruitful discussions.

Inclusive Idea Sharing
Encouraging everyone's input fosters inclusivity. Diverse ideas lead to innovative solutions.

Encouraging Risk-Taking and Experimentation:
Safe Environment for Risk-Taking

Fostering a risk-tolerant culture aids innovation. Failure acceptance drives experimentation.

Experimentation Platforms

Creating sandboxes for trials fosters creativity. Safe spaces encourage testing new ideas.

Agile Work Practices:
Agile Methodologies

Implementing agile frameworks aids collaboration. Iterative approaches enhance adaptability.

Flexible Work Structures

Offering flexibility drives creativity. Adaptive schedules promote individual productivity.

Recognition and Appreciation:
Celebrating Creativity

Recognizing innovative ideas boosts morale. Celebrating successes fosters a culture of innovation.

Rewarding Collaboration

Acknowledging team efforts drives motivation. Incentivizing teamwork encourages collaboration.

Encouraging Diverse Perspectives:
Inclusivity and Diversity

Fostering diverse teams drives innovation. Inclusive practices enhance problem-solving.

External Perspectives

Seeking external viewpoints aids creativity. Consultants or outside experts bring fresh insights.

Continuous Learning and Inspiration:
Learning Initiatives
Investing in skill development drives innovation. Learning opportunities enhance creativity.

Inspiration Platforms
Exposing teams to inspiring content fosters creativity. Creative outlets encourage fresh perspectives.

Conclusion
Collaboration and creativity serve as catalysts for innovation within digital agencies. By integrating collaborative workspaces, cross-functional collaboration, effective brainstorming, risk-taking encouragement, agile practices, recognition practices, diversity appreciation, continuous learning, and inspiration platforms, agencies can cultivate a culture of collaboration and creativity, driving innovation and competitiveness.

Strategies such as collaborative workspaces, cross-functional collaboration, effective brainstorming, risk-taking encouragement, agile practices, recognition practices, diversity appreciation, continuous learning, and inspiration platforms empower aspiring online agency owners to foster collaboration and nurture creativity, ensuring a dynamic and innovative environment for sustained success and growth.

Section 4: Chapter 7
Resolving Conflicts and Promoting Harmony

Conflict resolution and harmony within teams are critical for maintaining a productive and positive work environment within digital agencies. This chapter explores the significance of conflict resolution strategies, methodologies, and best practices essential for fostering harmony and resolving conflicts effectively within online agencies.

Importance of Conflict Resolution:
Maintaining Productivity
Effective conflict resolution minimizes disruptions. Resolving conflicts ensures workflow continuity.

Positive Work Environment

Addressing conflicts fosters positivity. Harmony enhances team morale and well-being.

Identifying Types of Conflicts:
Task-related Conflicts
Differences in work approach or goals. Resolution ensures alignment towards common objectives.

Interpersonal Conflicts
Personality clashes or communication issues. Addressing these enhances team cohesion.

Constructive Conflict Resolution:
Open Communication
Encouraging dialogue aids resolution. Transparent communication fosters understanding.

Active Listening
Understanding all viewpoints is crucial. Listening drives empathy and conflict understanding.

Conflict Resolution Techniques:
Mediation and Facilitation
Neutral mediators aid resolution. Facilitation ensures constructive discussions.

Negotiation Strategies
Finding common ground drives resolution. Win-win approaches ensure mutual satisfaction.

Establishing Conflict Resolution Procedures:
Clear Policies

Defining conflict resolution processes aids clarity. Guidelines ensure consistency in approach.

Role of Leadership
Leadership involvement ensures fairness. Guided interventions drive effective solutions.

Creating a Culture of Respect:
Respectful Communication
Encouraging respectful dialogues is vital. Constructive conversations aid conflict resolution.

Team-building Activities
Enhancing relationships fosters respect. Team activities build rapport and understanding.

Emotional Intelligence in Conflict Resolution:
Empathy and Understanding
Emotional awareness aids conflict resolution. Empathy drives better conflict understanding.

Self-regulation
Maintaining composure aids resolution. Emotion regulation ensures objective conflict handling.

Learning from Conflicts
Conflict Analysis
Understanding root causes aids prevention. Analyzing conflicts drives proactive solutions.

Continuous Improvement

Learning from conflicts enhances processes. Continuous learning fosters conflict resolution skills.

Promoting Harmony and Collaboration:
Celebrating Resolution

Acknowledging resolved conflicts boosts morale. Recognition fosters positive behaviors.

Collaboration Promotion

Encouraging teamwork minimizes conflicts. Collaboration drives understanding and harmony.

Conclusion

Conflict resolution and harmony are vital for the success of digital agencies. By integrating open communication, constructive conflict resolution techniques, established procedures, fostering respect, emotional intelligence, learning from conflicts, promoting harmony, and collaboration, agencies can cultivate an environment of understanding and collaboration, ensuring a positive and productive work culture.

Strategies such as open communication, constructive conflict resolution techniques, established procedures, fostering respect, emotional intelligence, learning from conflicts, promoting harmony, and collaboration empower aspiring online agency owners to effectively handle conflicts, foster harmony, and maintain a positive work environment conducive to growth and success.

Section 4: Chapter 8
Employee Engagement and Retention

Employee engagement and retention are crucial for the long-term success and growth of digital agencies. This chapter explores the significance of fostering employee engagement and implementing strategies essential for retaining top talent within online agencies.

Importance of Employee Engagement:
Productivity and Performance
Engaged employees drive productivity. High engagement levels correlate with better performance.

Enhanced Loyalty and Retention
Engaged employees are more likely to stay. Improved engagement reduces turnover rates.

Understanding Employee Engagement:

Employee Satisfaction

Satisfied employees are engaged. Addressing needs enhances satisfaction levels.

Emotional Connection with Work

A sense of purpose drives engagement. Aligning values fosters emotional investment in work.

Strategies for Employee Engagement

Clear Communication Channels

Open lines of communication foster engagement. Transparent communication builds trust.

Recognition and Appreciation

Acknowledging achievements boosts morale. Recognizing efforts drives motivation.

Providing Growth Opportunities

Learning and Development Programs

Investing in skill enhancement aids engagement. Training opportunities drive career growth.

Career Advancement Paths

Clear career trajectories motivate employees. Advancement opportunities retain talent.

Encouraging Work-Life Balance

Flexible Work Arrangements

Adapting to personal needs enhances satisfaction. Flexible hours support work-life balance.

Wellness Initiatives

Promoting well-being aids engagement. Wellness programs ensure employee health.

Fostering a Positive Work Culture:
Inclusive Environment

Diversity fosters engagement. Inclusive practices create a sense of belonging.

Trust and Empowerment

Empowering employees drives engagement. Trust ensures responsibility and autonomy.

Employee Feedback and Involvement:
Feedback Integration

Incorporating employee input enhances engagement. Addressing concerns fosters trust.

Involvement in Decision-Making

Involving employees in decisions drives engagement. Participation fosters commitment.

Recognition and Rewards Programs:
Performance-based Rewards

Rewarding achievements drives engagement. Incentives motivate exceptional performance.

Peer Recognition Initiatives

Acknowledging peer contributions boosts morale. Team recognition enhances engagement.

Managing Remote Employee Engagement:

Virtual Team-building Activities

Engaging remote teams fosters connections. Virtual events maintain team spirit.

Communication Tools

Utilizing digital platforms ensures connectivity. Effective tools aid engagement.

Measuring and Improving Engagement:
Employee Surveys

Gauging satisfaction aids improvement. Feedback guides strategies for enhancement.

Actionable Insights

Implementing changes based on feedback enhances engagement. Adaptation ensures relevance.

Conclusion

Employee engagement and retention are critical for the sustained success of digital agencies. By integrating clear communication, recognition and appreciation, growth opportunities, work-life balance, positive work culture, employee feedback involvement, recognition programs, remote engagement strategies, and continuous improvement, agencies can foster an engaged workforce, ensuring loyalty, productivity, and growth.

Strategies such as clear communication, recognition and appreciation, growth opportunities, work-life balance, positive work culture, employee feedback involvement, recognition programs, remote engagement strategies, and continuous improvement empower aspiring online agency owners to create an environment where employees feel valued, fostering engagement, retention, and sustained success.

Section 4: Chapter 9
Diversity and Inclusion in the Workplace

Diversity and inclusion are imperative for fostering innovation, creativity, and a positive work environment within digital agencies. This chapter explores the significance of embracing diversity and implementing strategies essential for creating an inclusive workplace culture within online agencies.

Importance of Diversity and Inclusion:
Innovation and Creativity
Diverse perspectives drive innovation. Inclusive cultures foster creative solutions and approaches.

Employee Well-being
Inclusive environments enhance morale. Diverse teams feel valued and included.

Understanding Diversity and Inclusion:

Diversity in Perspectives

Embracing differences enriches discussions. Varied viewpoints lead to comprehensive solutions.

Inclusive Environment

Creating a welcoming space fosters inclusion. Acceptance drives a sense of belonging.

Strategies for Fostering Diversity:

Diverse Hiring Practices

Prioritizing diversity in recruitment drives inclusion. Diverse talent pools enhance creativity.

Bias Awareness Training

Educating teams minimizes biases. Awareness ensures fair treatment and opportunities.

Cultivating an Inclusive Culture

Inclusive Policies

Implementing fair policies ensures inclusion. Guidelines promote equality in the workplace.

Leadership Role in Inclusion

Leadership sets the tone for inclusion. Support drives a culture of acceptance.

Empowering Employee Resource Groups:

Diverse Affinity Groups

Creating forums for diverse groups fosters inclusion. Forums provide support and representation.

Involving ERGs in Decision-Making
Including ERGs in discussions enhances inclusion. Representation aids in diverse perspectives.

Building Bridges Across Differences:
Cultural Competency Training
Understanding diverse cultures drives inclusion. Learning about differences enhances cohesion.

Cross-cultural Collaboration
Encouraging teamwork across cultures aids inclusion. Collaboration bridges cultural gaps.

Addressing Unconscious Bias:
Unconscious Bias Training
Addressing biases ensures fairness. Awareness drives conscious decisions.

Fair Performance Evaluations
Ensuring impartial evaluations aids inclusion. Merit-based assessments promote fairness.

Celebrating Diversity:
Cultural Celebrations
Acknowledging cultural events fosters inclusion. Celebrations promote understanding.

Diversity Appreciation Programs
Recognizing diverse contributions boosts morale. Inclusivity programs foster a sense of belonging.

Measuring and Improving Inclusion:

Diversity Metrics
Tracking diversity aids improvement. Metrics guide strategies for enhancement.

Employee Feedback
Gauging inclusion aids improvement. Addressing concerns ensures an inclusive culture.

Conclusion
Diversity and inclusion are fundamental for the success of digital agencies. By integrating diverse hiring practices, bias awareness training, inclusive policies, leadership support, employee resource groups, cultural competency, addressing unconscious bias, celebrating diversity, and continuous improvement, agencies can foster an inclusive workplace culture, ensuring innovation, fairness, and employee well-being.

Strategies such as diverse hiring practices, bias awareness training, inclusive policies, leadership support, employee resource groups, cultural competency, addressing unconscious bias, celebrating diversity, and continuous improvement empower aspiring online agency owners to create an environment that values differences, fosters inclusion, and drives success through diverse perspectives.

Section 4: Chapter 10
Empowering and Motivating Your Team

Empowerment and motivation are essential elements for driving productivity, innovation, and a high-performance culture within digital agencies. This chapter explores the significance of empowering and motivating teams, strategies, methodologies, and best practices essential for cultivating a motivated and empowered workforce within online agencies.

Importance of Empowerment and Motivation:
Enhanced Performance

Empowered teams drive productivity. Motivated employees produce exceptional results.

Creativity and Innovation

Empowerment fosters creative solutions. Motivated teams drive innovation.

Understanding Empowerment:
Delegating Authority

Empowering teams aids ownership. Delegating responsibilities fosters accountability.

Providing Resources and Support

Equipping teams ensures success. Support drives confidence and initiative.

Strategies for Empowerment
Clear Vision and Goals

Aligning teams to a shared vision aids empowerment. Clear objectives drive motivation.

Trust and Autonomy

Granting autonomy fosters empowerment. Trust ensures accountability and initiative.

Fostering a Motivational Environment:
Recognition and Rewards

Acknowledging achievements boosts morale. Rewards drive motivation and effort.

Encouraging Creativity

Providing outlets for creativity aids motivation. Creative opportunities drive engagement.

Developing Leadership Skills:
Coaching and Mentorship

Offering guidance aids development. Mentorship programs drive skill enhancement.

Leadership Opportunities

Providing leadership roles empowers employees. Opportunities foster growth.

Building a Supportive Culture:
Collaborative Environment

Teamwork enhances motivation. Collaboration drives collective success.

Open Communication

Transparent dialogue fosters empowerment. Openness ensures trust and understanding.

Encouraging Continuous Learning:
Learning Opportunities

Investing in skill development drives motivation. Learning aids growth and adaptability.

Growth Paths

Clear career trajectories motivate employees. Advancement opportunities retain talent.

Incentivizing Performance:
Performance-Based Incentives

Rewarding exceptional performance boosts morale. Incentives drive goal attainment.

Team-based Rewards

Recognizing team efforts fosters camaraderie. Team incentives drive collaboration.

Addressing Employee Needs:
Wellness Initiatives

Promoting well-being aids motivation. Wellness programs ensure employee health.

Work-Life Balance

Supporting personal needs enhances satisfaction. Balance aids in employee well-being.

Measuring Team Empowerment and Motivation:
Feedback and Surveys

Gauging satisfaction aids improvement. Feedback guides strategies for enhancement.

Metrics for Performance

Tracking productivity ensures improvement. Metrics guide strategies for empowerment.

Conclusion

Empowerment and motivation are crucial for the success of digital agencies. By integrating clear goals, autonomy, recognition, supportive cultures, leadership development, continuous learning, performance incentives, addressing employee needs, and measurement strategies, agencies can cultivate a motivated and empowered workforce, ensuring productivity, innovation, and sustained success.

Strategies such as clear goals, autonomy, recognition, supportive cultures, leadership development, continuous learning, performance incentives, addressing employee needs, and measurement strategies empower aspiring online agency owners to create an environment that values and empowers employees, fostering motivation, empowerment, and sustained success.

Section 5: Chapter 1
Scaling Your Online Agency Effectively

Scaling an online agency is a critical phase that requires strategic planning, resource allocation, and effective management. This chapter explores the significance of scaling and strategies essential for expanding and growing an online agency effectively.

Importance of Scaling Effectively:
Meeting Growing Demands
Scaling accommodates increased demand. Expansion ensures meeting client needs.

Competitive Edge
Effective scaling drives competitiveness. Growth solidifies market position.

Understanding Scaling in Digital Agencies:
Scalability in Operations

Adapting to increased workloads aids scalability. Processes ensure seamless growth.

Resource Allocation

Optimizing resources drives scalability. Efficient allocation ensures sustainable growth.

Strategies for Effective Scaling
Clear Growth Plan

Setting growth objectives aids scaling. Defined strategies guide expansion.

Technology Integration

Utilizing scalable tech aids growth. Automation ensures efficiency in scaling.

Building a Scalable Infrastructure:
Scalable Systems

Implementing adaptable systems aids scaling. Flexibility ensures operational growth.

Agile Frameworks

Utilizing agile methodologies aids scalability. Iterative approaches drive adaptability.

Expanding Human Capital:
Talent Acquisition

Scaling requires a skilled workforce. Hiring drives capability expansion.

Training and Development

Investing in employee skills aids scaling. Skill enhancement ensures competency.

Leveraging Partnerships and Networks:
Strategic Collaborations

Partnerships drive resource access. Collaborations aid scaling initiatives.

Networking and Alliances

Building industry connections aids scaling. Alliances drive growth opportunities.

Financial Management for Scaling:
Efficient Budgeting

Strategic financial planning drives scaling. Budgets ensure resource optimization.

Funding Opportunities

Accessing capital aids expansion. Funding drives scalability initiatives.

Measuring and Assessing Scalability:
Performance Metrics

Tracking performance guides scaling. Metrics aid in evaluating growth.

Adaptability and Flexibility

Assessing adaptability ensures scalability. Flexibility drives growth potential.

Challenges and Mitigation Strategies:

Overcoming Growth Pains

Scaling challenges require proactive solutions. Mitigation strategies ensure progress.

Risk Assessment

Identifying risks aids mitigation. Preparedness minimizes scalability challenges.

Continuous Innovation for Scaling:
Innovation Initiatives

Fostering creativity drives growth. Innovation ensures a competitive edge.

Adaptation to Market Changes

Anticipating trends aids scalability. Adaptation drives sustained growth.

Conclusion

Scaling effectively is crucial for the long-term success of digital agencies. By integrating clear growth plans, technology integration, scalable infrastructure, human capital expansion, partnerships, financial management, measurement strategies, mitigation strategies, innovation initiatives, and market adaptation, agencies can scale their operations effectively, ensuring competitiveness and sustained growth.

Strategies such as clear growth plans, technology integration, scalable infrastructure, human capital expansion, partnerships, financial management, measurement strategies, mitigation strategies, innovation initiatives, and market adaptation empower aspiring online agency owners to navigate the complexities of scaling, fostering expansion and competitiveness in the digital landscape.

Section 5: Chapter 2
Expanding Your Services and Offerings

Diversifying services and offerings is pivotal for the growth and competitiveness of online agencies. This chapter delves into the significance of expanding services and strategies essential for broadening the service portfolio within digital agencies.

Importance of Service Expansion:
Meeting Client Needs
Diversification caters to varied demands. Expanded services ensure comprehensive solutions.

Competitive Edge
Widening service offerings drives competitiveness. Expansion solidifies market position.

Understanding Service Expansion:

Market Research

Identifying gaps aids service expansion. Research ensures relevance in new offerings.

Client Feedback

Listening to client needs guides expansion. Feedback ensures alignment with market demands.

Strategies for Expanding Services:

Assessing Core Competencies

Leveraging strengths in service expansion drives success. Capitalizing on expertise aids diversification.

Identifying Market Trends

Anticipating trends guides service expansion. Adaptation ensures relevance in new offerings.

Introducing New Service Lines:

Iterative Approach

Gradual introduction minimizes risks. Phased expansions ensure controlled growth.

Innovation in Offerings

Creativity drives new services. Innovative solutions attract clients and drive expansion.

Partnering and Collaboration:

Strategic Alliances

Partnerships aid service diversification. Collaborations ensure access to new markets.

Acquiring Specialized Expertise

Mergers or acquisitions drive service expansion. Accessing expertise aids diversification.

Testing New Offerings:
Pilot Programs

Testing services ensures viability. Pilots aid in refining offerings before full-scale launch.

Client Beta Testing

Involving clients validates services. Feedback drives improvements pre-launch.

Marketing and Promoting New Services:
Tailored Marketing Strategies

Promoting new services drives visibility. Tailored approaches attract target audiences.

Client Education

Educating clients on new offerings ensures adoption. Awareness drives service utilization.

Measuring Service Expansion Success:
Performance Metrics

Tracking service success aids improvement. Metrics guide strategies for enhancement.

Client Satisfaction

Client feedback gauges service relevance. Satisfaction ensures service adoption.

Challenges in Service Expansion:

Managing Resources

Allocating resources for expansion is crucial. Resource management minimizes challenges.

Market Acceptance

Acceptance of new services requires time. Patience ensures gradual adoption.

Continuous Innovation in Services:
R&D Initiatives

Investing in R&D drives service innovation. Continuous improvement aids competitiveness.

Adaptability to Changing Needs

Adapting to market changes ensures relevance. Flexibility drives sustained growth.

Conclusion

Expanding services and offerings is vital for the long-term success of digital agencies. By integrating market research, client feedback, core competency assessment, trend identification, iterative approaches, partnerships, testing strategies, marketing efforts, measurement strategies, addressing challenges, continuous innovation, and adaptability, agencies can diversify their service portfolio effectively, ensuring competitiveness and sustained growth.

Strategies such as market research, client feedback, core competency assessment, trend identification, iterative approaches, partnerships, testing strategies, marketing efforts, measurement strategies, addressing challenges, continuous innovation, and adaptability empower aspiring online agency owners to expand their service offerings, driving growth and maintaining relevance in the ever-evolving digital landscape.

Section 5: Chapter 3
Globalization and International Markets

Expanding into global markets presents tremendous opportunities for growth and diversification for online agencies. This chapter explores the significance of globalization and strategies essential for entering and succeeding in international markets within digital agencies.

Importance of Globalization:
Market Expansion
Globalization broadens the customer base. Access to international markets drives growth.

Diversification
Entering global markets minimizes dependency. Diversification ensures resilience.

Understanding International Markets:

Market Research

Understanding cultural nuances aids market entry. Research ensures relevance in new markets.

Legal and Regulatory Compliance

Adhering to international laws ensures legitimacy. Compliance minimizes risks in new markets.

Strategies for Global Expansion:

Target Market Identification

Selecting suitable markets aids entry. Targeted approaches ensure focused expansion.

Cultural Adaptation

Adapting to cultural differences drives success. Localization ensures market acceptance.

Entry Modes and Strategies:

Exporting and Importing

Entry through trade ensures market access. Importing drives product diversity.

Joint Ventures and Partnerships

Collaborations aid market entry. Partnerships ensure localized expertise.

Establishing a Global Presence:

Online Platforms

Utilizing digital channels ensures visibility. Online presence drives global reach.

Physical Presence

Establishing offices aids market penetration. Local presence drives trust and credibility.

Addressing Language and Communication:
Multilingual Services

Language adaptation ensures inclusivity. Multilingual communication drives engagement.

Cross-Cultural Communication

Understanding cultural nuances aids interactions. Effective communication ensures acceptance.

Financial Considerations:
Currency Management

Managing currency fluctuations minimizes risks. Financial planning ensures stability.

International Taxation

Understanding tax laws ensures compliance. Tax planning minimizes financial hurdles.

Measuring International Success:
Market Penetration

Tracking market share aids improvement. Metrics guide strategies for expansion.

Customer Satisfaction

Client feedback gauges market acceptance. Satisfaction drives market retention.

Challenges in Globalization:

Cultural Misunderstandings

Overcoming cultural barriers requires adaptation. Understanding ensures smooth operations.

Regulatory Compliance

Navigating international laws is complex. Legal support minimizes compliance challenges.

Continuous Adaptation in Global Markets:

Market Analysis

Constant market evaluation aids adaptation. Adaptability ensures competitiveness.

Innovation in Offerings

Continuous improvement drives acceptance. Innovation ensures market relevance.

Conclusion

Globalization and entry into international markets present opportunities for exponential growth for digital agencies. By integrating market research, legal compliance, target market identification, cultural adaptation, entry strategies, global presence establishment, communication focus, financial planning, measurement strategies, addressing challenges, continuous adaptation, and innovation, agencies can successfully penetrate global markets, ensuring growth and competitiveness.

Strategies such as market research, legal compliance, target market identification, cultural adaptation, entry strategies, global presence establishment, communication focus, financial planning, measurement strategies, addressing challenges, continuous adaptation, and innovation empower aspiring online agency owners to navigate global expansion, fostering success and sustainability in the global business landscape.

Section 5: Chapter 4
Strategic Partnerships and Alliances

Strategic partnerships and alliances play a pivotal role in the growth and success of online agencies. This chapter explores the significance of fostering strategic partnerships and strategies essential for forming successful alliances within digital agencies.

Importance of Strategic Partnerships:
Access to Resources
Partnerships provide access to new resources. Collaboration ensures mutual benefit.

Market Expansion
Alliances aid in entering new markets. Partnerships broaden the customer base.

Understanding Strategic Partnerships:
Alignment of Goals
Shared objectives drive successful partnerships. Alignment ensures mutual growth.

Complementary Strengths
Leveraging each other's strengths drives success. Complementarity ensures synergy.

Strategies for Forming Alliances:
Identifying Synergy
Matching objectives ensures fit. Synergy drives successful collaborations.

Due Diligence in Selection
Thorough assessment minimizes risks. Research ensures compatibility in partnerships.

Types of Strategic Partnerships:
Supplier and Vendor Partnerships
Supplier relationships ensure resource access. Vendors aid in service delivery.

Joint Marketing Ventures
Collaborative marketing drives visibility. Joint campaigns enhance market reach.

Establishing Long-Term Partnerships:
Clear Communication
Open dialogue fosters successful alliances. Transparent communication ensures trust.

Mutual Benefit Focus

Ensuring mutual benefits drives partnerships. Win-win approaches foster sustainability.

Managing Partner Relationships:
Relationship Maintenance

Nurturing partnerships drives success. Relationship management ensures longevity.

Conflict Resolution Mechanisms

Addressing disputes ensures sustainability. Conflict resolution drives alliance stability.

Leveraging Technology in Partnerships:
Collaborative Tools

Utilizing shared platforms aids communication. Technology ensures connectivity.

Data Sharing and Integration

Information exchange drives efficiency. Integrated systems ensure seamless operations.

Measuring Partnership Success:
Performance Metrics

Tracking alliance success aids improvement. Metrics guide strategies for enhancement.

Feedback and Reviews

Evaluating partnership experience drives improvements. Feedback ensures mutual growth.

Challenges in Partnerships:

Misalignment in Objectives
Aligning goals is crucial. Shared vision ensures partnership success.

Cultural Differences
Overcoming cultural barriers requires adaptation. Understanding drives collaboration.

Continuous Evolution in Partnerships:
Regular Evaluation
Assessing partnerships aids adaptation. Continuous improvement ensures relevance.

Innovation in Collaboration
Fostering creativity drives alliance success. Innovation ensures market competitiveness.

Conclusion
Strategic partnerships and alliances are instrumental for the growth and sustainability of digital agencies. By integrating synergy identification, due diligence, long-term focus, relationship management, technological leverage, measurement strategies, addressing challenges, continuous evolution, and innovation in collaborations, agencies can foster successful alliances, ensuring mutual growth and market competitiveness.

Strategies such as synergy identification, due diligence, long-term focus, relationship management, technological leverage, measurement strategies, addressing challenges, continuous evolution, and innovation in collaborations empower aspiring online agency owners to form and maintain successful partnerships, fostering growth and sustainability in a competitive business landscape.

Section 5: Chapter 5
Mergers, Acquisitions, and Growth Strategies

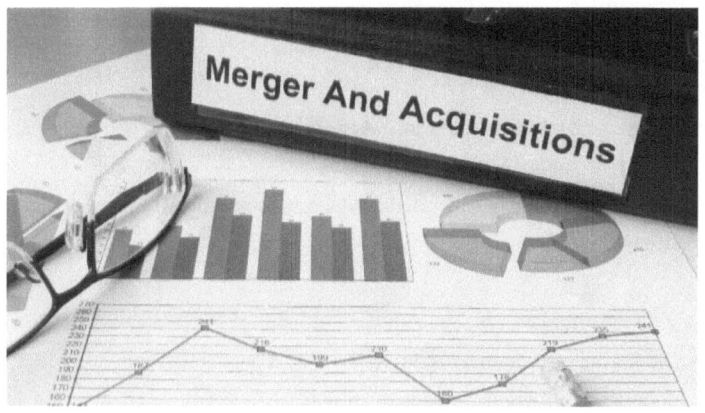

Mergers and acquisitions (M&A) present strategic opportunities for growth and expansion for online agencies. This chapter explores the significance of M&A activities and growth strategies essential for scaling and evolving within digital agencies.

Importance of Mergers and Acquisitions:
Rapid Expansion
M&A expedite growth and market penetration. Acquisitions ensure quick market access.

Access to Resources
Mergers provide access to new assets. Acquisitions ensure resource enhancement.

Understanding Mergers and Acquisitions:
Mergers for Synergy

Combining forces drive success. Merging entities ensure mutual benefit.

Acquisitions for Growth

Purchasing assets ensures expansion. Acquisitions drive market dominance.

Strategies for Mergers and Acquisitions:
Target Identification

Selecting suitable entities aids M&A success. Identifying potential ensures synergy.

Due Diligence

Thorough assessment minimizes risks. Research ensures compatibility in mergers/acquisitions.

Types of Growth Strategies:
Horizontal Integration

Merging with competitors drives market dominance. Horizontal growth ensures expansion.

Vertical Integration

Acquiring suppliers or distributors aids control. Vertical growth ensures resource control.

Implementing M&A Strategies:
Negotiation and Deal Structuring

Strategic negotiations drive successful deals. Structuring ensures mutual benefit.

Integration Planning

Smooth integration ensures success. Planning minimizes disruption in operations.

Risks and Challenges:
Cultural Differences

Merging organizational cultures requires adaptation. Understanding drives collaboration.

Integration Complexities

Merging operations requires coordination. Planning minimizes integration challenges.

Leveraging Synergies:
Operational Efficiencies

Consolidating operations drives efficiency. Synergies ensure cost savings.

Complementary Resources

Utilizing combined assets drives growth. Resources ensure enhanced capabilities.

Measuring M&A Success:
Financial Performance

Tracking financial metrics aids assessment. Performance metrics guide improvement.

Cultural Integration

Evaluating cultural alignment ensures success. Integration fosters collaboration.

Continuous Growth Strategies:

Diversification Efforts

Expanding service lines ensures resilience. Diversification drives market relevance.

Innovation Initiatives

Fostering creativity drives growth. Innovation ensures competitive advantage.

Conclusion

Mergers, acquisitions, and growth strategies are pivotal for the expansion and sustainability of digital agencies. By integrating target identification, due diligence, integration planning, leveraging synergies, addressing challenges, measurement strategies, continuous growth initiatives, and innovation, agencies can effectively utilize M&A strategies for growth and market dominance.

Strategies such as target identification, due diligence, integration planning, leveraging synergies, addressing challenges, measurement strategies, continuous growth initiatives, and innovation empower aspiring online agency owners to strategize M&A activities, fostering growth and sustainability in the dynamic business landscape.

Section 5: Chapter 6
Managing Finances During Growth Phases

Effective financial management is critical during growth phases to sustain and leverage expansion opportunities for online agencies. This chapter explores the significance of financial management and strategies essential for managing finances during periods of growth within digital agencies.

Importance of Financial Management:
Sustainable Growth

Efficient financial management ensures sustainability. Growth requires fiscal responsibility.

Resource Allocation

Proper allocation drives expansion. Financial planning ensures optimal resource use.

Understanding Financial Management:
Budgeting and Forecasting

Strategic budgeting guides growth. Forecasting minimizes financial uncertainties.

Cash Flow Management

Managing cash ensures liquidity. Cash flow drives operations during expansion.

Strategies for Financial Management:
Financial Planning

Strategic planning guides growth initiatives. Plans ensure resource optimization.

Cost Control Measures

Minimizing unnecessary spending aids growth. Cost control drives fiscal efficiency.

Funding Options for Growth:
Internal Financing

Utilizing profits for expansion ensures control. Internal funds aid organic growth.

External Financing

Accessing capital ensures rapid expansion. Loans/investments drive quick growth.

Risk Management in Finance:
Contingency Planning

Planning for unforeseen events minimizes risks. Preparedness ensures continuity.

Diversification of Investments

Spreading investments minimizes risks. Diversification ensures financial stability.

Scaling Financial Systems:
Upgrade Financial Tools

Utilizing advanced tools aids growth tracking. Technology ensures scalability.

Compliance and Reporting

Adhering to regulations ensures legitimacy. Reporting drives transparency in growth.

Measuring Financial Success:
Key Performance Indicators (KPIs)

Tracking financial metrics aids assessment. KPIs guide strategies for improvement.

Return on Investment (ROI)

Evaluating returns ensures growth effectiveness. ROI measures expansion outcomes.

Challenges in Financial Management:
Cash Flow Pressures

Managing cash during growth is challenging. Forecasting minimizes cash flow gaps.

Overinvestment Risks

Excessive spending may risk sustainability. Balance ensures measured growth.

Continuous Financial Evolution:

Periodic Reviews
Assessing financial health drives improvement. Reviews guide fiscal strategies.

Adaptation to Market Changes
Anticipating market shifts aids financial stability. Adaptation ensures resilience.

Conclusion
Effective financial management during growth phases is crucial for the sustainability and success of digital agencies. By integrating strategic planning, cost control measures, funding options, risk management, scaling financial systems, measurement strategies, addressing challenges, continuous financial evolution, and adaptation, agencies can manage finances effectively during growth, ensuring sustainability and expansion.

Strategies such as strategic planning, cost control measures, funding options, risk management, scaling financial systems, measurement strategies, addressing challenges, continuous financial evolution, and adaptation empower aspiring online agency owners to navigate growth phases, fostering fiscal responsibility and sustainability in a competitive business landscape.

Section 5: Chapter 7
Creating a Legacy and Long-Term Vision

Establishing a legacy and crafting a long-term vision are crucial aspects for the enduring success and impact of online agencies. This chapter explores the significance of creating a legacy and strategies essential for fostering a long-term vision within digital agencies.

Importance of Creating a Legacy:
Enduring Impact
A legacy transcends time. It ensures the agency's long-term relevance and influence.

Cultural Significance
A strong legacy fosters an agency's identity. It drives values and shapes perceptions.

Understanding Legacy Creation:
Visionary Leadership

Leadership drives legacy creation. Vision ensures agency continuity.

Organizational Culture

Cultural values ensure legacy sustainability. Culture drives long-term impact.

Strategies for Legacy Building:
Defining Core Values

Establishing values drives legacy creation. Core principles guide long-term actions.

Talent Development

Investing in talent ensures legacy continuity. Skill enhancement fosters sustainability.

Long-Term Vision Crafting:
Vision Clarity

Defining a clear vision guides actions. A strong vision drives long-term strategies.

Adaptability and Innovation

Adaptation ensures vision relevance. Innovation sustains long-term impact.

Embracing Corporate Social Responsibility:
Ethical Practices

Ethical conduct shapes legacy. Responsibility drives agency reputation.

Social Impact Initiatives

Community engagement aids legacy creation. Social impact ensures agency contribution.

Measuring Legacy and Long-Term Vision:
Impact Assessment

Evaluating legacy impact aids improvement. Measurement guides strategic alignment.

Vision Alignment

Ensuring actions align with the vision. Alignment drives long-term agency goals.

Challenges in Legacy Creation:
Succession Planning

Continuity in leadership is vital. Succession plans ensure legacy sustainability.

Evolving Market Dynamics

Adapting to changes is challenging. Agility ensures legacy relevance.

Continuous Evolution of Vision:
Periodic Vision Reviews

Assessing vision alignment drives improvement. Reviews guide strategic adaptation.

Innovation and Adaptation

Continuous improvement ensures legacy relevance. Innovation sustains impact.

Conclusion

Creating a legacy and fostering a long-term vision are essential for the sustained impact and enduring success of digital agencies. By integrating visionary leadership, organizational culture, core values, talent development, long-term vision crafting, CSR initiatives, measurement strategies, addressing challenges, continuous evolution of vision, and innovation, agencies can create a lasting legacy and drive a meaningful long-term impact.

Strategies such as visionary leadership, organizational culture, core values, talent development, long-term vision crafting, CSR initiatives, measurement strategies, addressing challenges, continuous evolution of vision, and innovation empower aspiring online agency owners to establish a legacy and long-term vision, fostering sustained impact and relevance in the dynamic business landscape.

Section 5: Chapter 8
Innovating for Sustainable Growth

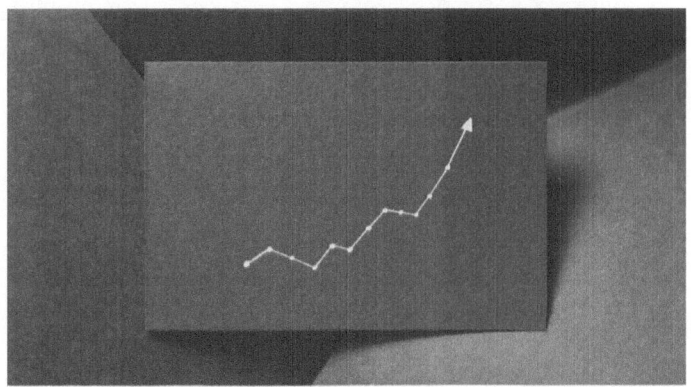

Innovation serves as a catalyst for sustained growth and competitiveness within online agencies. This chapter explores the significance of innovation and strategies essential for fostering innovation to ensure sustainable growth within digital agencies.

Importance of Innovation:
Competitive Advantage
Innovation drives competitiveness. Unique solutions ensure market differentiation.

Adaptation to Change
Innovation aids in adapting to market shifts. Flexibility ensures sustained relevance.

Understanding Innovation:
Culture of Creativity

Fostering a culture of creativity drives innovation. A conducive environment ensures ideation.

Continuous Improvement

Iterative processes ensure innovation. Continuous refinement drives growth.

Strategies for Fostering Innovation:
Encouraging Idea Generation

Promoting idea sharing drives innovation. Encouragement fosters a culture of creativity.

Experimentation and Risk-Taking

Embracing experimentation drives innovation. Risk-taking ensures breakthroughs.

Implementing Innovative Practices:
Agile Methodologies

Utilizing agile frameworks aids innovation. Iterative approaches drive adaptability.

Technology Integration

Leveraging technology fosters innovation. Automation ensures efficiency in innovation processes.

Innovation in Service Offerings:
Creative Solutions

Innovative services attract clients. Creativity ensures service differentiation.

Customer-Centric Innovation

Understanding client needs drives innovation. Client feedback ensures relevance.

Measuring Innovation Success:
Impact Assessment
Evaluating innovation impact drives improvement. Measurement guides strategic alignment.

ROI in Innovation
Assessing returns ensures innovation effectiveness. ROI measures innovation outcomes.

Challenges in Innovation:
Resistance to Change
Overcoming inertia is challenging. Encouragement drives innovative culture adoption.

Resource Constraints
Managing limited resources hampers innovation. Creativity ensures resource optimization.

Continuous Evolution in Innovation:
Periodic Innovation Reviews
Assessing innovation strategies aids adaptation. Reviews guide strategic improvements.
Adaptability to Market Dynamics
Anticipating shifts ensures innovation relevance. Adaptation drives sustained growth.

Conclusion
Innovation is a driving force for sustainable growth and competitiveness in digital agencies. By integrating a culture of

creativity, continuous improvement, idea generation, experimentation, innovative practices, measurement strategies, addressing challenges, continuous evolution in innovation, and adaptability, agencies can foster innovation for sustainable growth.

Strategies such as a culture of creativity, continuous improvement, idea generation, experimentation, innovative practices, measurement strategies, addressing challenges, continuous evolution in innovation, and adaptability empower aspiring online agency owners to drive innovation, fostering sustained growth and competitiveness in a dynamic business landscape.

Section 5: Chapter 9
Adapting to Changing Industry Landscapes

The ability to adapt to evolving industry landscapes is crucial for the sustained success and relevance of online agencies. This chapter explores the significance of adaptation and strategies essential for navigating and thriving amidst changing industry landscapes within digital agencies.

Importance of Adaptation:
Market Relevance
Adaptation ensures continued relevance. Flexibility drives competitiveness.

Survival in Dynamic Markets
Evolving industries require adaptability. Resilience ensures agency survival.

Understanding Adaptation:

Market Analysis

Constant analysis aids adaptation. Understanding shifts ensures strategic changes.

Agility and Flexibility

Agility drives adaptation. Flexibility ensures responsiveness to market shifts.

Strategies for Adaptation:

Proactive Planning

Anticipating changes drives adaptation. Proactivity ensures preparedness.

Scalable Systems and Processes

Scalability aids agility. Flexible systems ensure quick adaptation.

Embracing Technological Advances:

Technology Integration

Utilizing cutting-edge tech aids adaptation. Tech ensures industry relevance.

Automation and AI Integration

Leveraging automation drives efficiency. AI ensures predictive adaptations.

Industry-Specific Adaptation:

Regulatory Compliance

Adhering to evolving regulations is crucial. Compliance ensures legality.

Trend Analysis

Analyzing industry trends guides adaptation. Trend anticipation ensures alignment.

Measuring Adaptation Success:
Market Penetration

Tracking market presence aids assessment. Penetration measures adaptation impact.

Customer Satisfaction

Client feedback gauges adaptation relevance. Satisfaction ensures market retention.

Challenges in Adaptation:
Resistance to Change

Overcoming inertia impedes adaptation. Culture drives change acceptance.

Resource Constraints

Limited resources hinder adaptation efforts. Optimization ensures adaptability.

Continuous Evolution in Adaptation:
Periodic Industry Assessments

Evaluating industry shifts aids adaptation. Assessment drives strategic changes.

Flexibility in Strategy

Adaptability ensures strategy relevance. Flexibility drives sustained adaptation.

Conclusion

Adapting to changing industry landscapes is pivotal for the sustained success of digital agencies. By integrating proactive planning, scalable systems, technological integration, industry-specific adaptation, measurement strategies, addressing challenges, continuous evolution in adaptation, and flexibility, agencies can navigate industry shifts and ensure sustained relevance.

Strategies such as proactive planning, scalable systems, technological integration, industry-specific adaptation, measurement strategies, addressing challenges, continuous evolution in adaptation, and flexibility empower aspiring online agency owners to adapt to changing industry landscapes, fostering sustained relevance and competitiveness in a dynamic business environment.

Section 5: Chapter 10
Reflections on Building an Empire

The journey of building an empire within the realm of online agencies is a testament to perseverance, innovation, and strategic acumen. This chapter serves as a reflective exploration, delving into the pivotal aspects and key takeaways for aspiring entrepreneurs aiming to build their own digital empires.

Reflecting on the Journey:
Visionary Leadership
Leadership drives empire-building. Vision ensures direction and purpose.

Resilience in Challenges
Overcoming obstacles shapes success. Resilience ensures perseverance.

Key Aspects in Empire Building:

Customer-Centric Approach

Putting clients at the forefront drives success. Customer satisfaction ensures loyalty.

Innovation and Adaptation

Embracing innovation ensures relevance. Adaptation drives sustainability.

Lessons from Successes and Failures:
Learning from Failures

Failures offer valuable insights. Learning ensures continuous improvement.

Celebrating Successes

Acknowledging achievements drives motivation. Successes propel further growth.

Ethical Responsibility:
Social Impact Initiatives

Contributing to society fosters goodwill. Responsibility ensures positive impact.

Sustainable Business Practices

Ethical conduct ensures long-term success. Sustainability drives ethical growth.

Scaling Challenges and Solutions:
Team Building and Leadership

Building strong teams drives scalability. Leadership ensures team cohesion.

Operational Scalability

Efficiency drives scalability. Optimization ensures growth readiness.

Vision and Legacy:
Long-Term Vision Crafting
Crafting a vision ensures enduring impact. Long-term goals guide empire-building.

Legacy Creation
Establishing a legacy ensures agency identity. Cultural values shape lasting impact.

Evolution in the Industry:
Industry Trends and Adaptation
Adapting to market shifts drives success. Agility ensures industry relevance.

Technology Integration
Leveraging tech fosters growth. Automation ensures operational efficiency.

Continuous Improvement:
Innovation Culture
Fostering creativity drives growth. Innovation ensures sustained relevance.

Learning and Development
Investing in skill enhancement drives growth. Knowledge ensures competitiveness.

Conclusion

Reflections on building an empire within the domain of online agencies underscore the pivotal elements of visionary leadership, customer-centricity, innovation, ethical responsibility, scalability challenges, long-term vision, industry evolution, and continuous improvement. Embracing these aspects empowers aspiring entrepreneurs to embark on their journeys toward building digital empires.

The reflections offered in this chapter serve as a compass, guiding aspiring online agency owners towards the foundational principles and essential elements required to navigate the complexities and challenges of building a thriving digital empire.

The comprehensive journey of building an empire within the online agency landscape embodies a dynamic amalgamation of vision, adaptability, resilience, ethical responsibility, and continuous innovation, all of which converge to carve out a lasting legacy and foster sustained growth.

Section 6: Chapter 1
The Power of Automation in Digital Business

In the digital realm, automation stands as a transformative force, reshaping how businesses operate, streamline processes, and enhance productivity. This chapter explores the profound impact and strategies essential for leveraging automation in the landscape of digital agencies.

Understanding Automation:
Definition and Scope

Automation involves using technology to execute tasks without human intervention. Its scope encompasses various business functions.

Evolution and Adoption

The evolution of automation has revolutionized industries. Adoption ensures efficiency gains.

Significance of Automation in Digital Business:
Efficiency and Productivity
Automation drives efficiency gains. Increased productivity ensures competitive advantage.

Resource Optimization
Streamlining processes saves time and resources. Optimization aids in scaling operations.

Automation Across Business Functions:
Marketing Automation
Automated marketing drives targeted campaigns. Personalization ensures engagement.

Workflow Automation
Streamlining workflows ensures operational efficiency. Automation reduces manual tasks.

Leveraging Cutting-Edge Automation:
AI and Machine Learning
Utilizing AI enhances decision-making. Machine learning aids in predictive analytics.

Robotic Process Automation (RPA)
Automating repetitive tasks drives efficiency. RPA ensures process optimization.

Automation in Lead Generation:
Lead Scoring and Nurturing

Automated lead scoring aids in prioritization. Nurturing drives conversion rates.

Chatbots and Customer Support
Automated chatbots ensure 24/7 support. Customer service is streamlined via automation.

The Role of Automation in Social Media:
Social Media Management
Automated scheduling ensures consistent posting. Analytics aid in strategy refinement.

Community Engagement
Automated responses drive engagement. Interaction ensures brand presence.

Creative Design Automation:
Template-Based Design

Utilizing design templates aids efficiency. Automated design tools streamline processes.

Personalized Content Generation
Automation aids in content creation. Personalization ensures audience engagement.

The Impact of Automation on Workforce:
Skill Enhancement and Redeployment
Automation leads to new skill demands. Upskilling ensures workforce adaptation.

Human-Automation Collaboration

Augmenting human efforts drives innovation. Collaboration ensures synergy.

Challenges in Automation Implementation:
Integration Complexity

Integrating various tools requires expertise. Seamless integration drives efficiency.

Resistance to Change

Overcoming reluctance is challenging. Training ensures adoption success.

Measuring Automation Success:
Efficiency Metrics

Tracking process improvements guides assessment. Metrics ensure optimization.

Cost Reduction and ROI

Evaluating cost savings aids analysis. ROI measures automation effectiveness.

Future Trends in Automation
Hyperautomation

Integrating various automation technologies drives efficiency. Hyperautomation ensures seamless operations.

Autonomous Agents

AI-driven autonomous agents aid decision-making. Autonomy ensures operational fluidity.

Conclusion

The transformative power of automation in digital business is reshaping how agencies operate, innovate, and compete. By integrating efficiency gains, resource optimization, cutting-edge automation technologies, lead generation, social media management, creative design automation, workforce adaptation, addressing challenges, measuring success, and future trends, agencies can harness automation for sustained growth and competitiveness.

Strategies such as embracing efficiency gains, resource optimization, cutting-edge technologies, lead generation, social media management, creative design automation, workforce adaptation, addressing challenges, measuring success, and exploring future trends empower aspiring online agency owners to harness automation's potential, fostering growth and resilience in an ever-evolving digital landscape.

Section 6: Chapter 2
ChatGPT Technology and Its
Applications in Marketing

ChatGPT technology, a powerful form of AI-driven conversational agents, has emerged as a pivotal tool in revolutionizing marketing strategies within the digital landscape. This chapter explores the profound impact and diverse applications of ChatGPT technology in modern marketing for digital agencies.

Understanding ChatGPT Technology:
Definition and Functionality
ChatGPT technology employs AI to facilitate human-like conversation. It interprets queries and generates contextually relevant responses.

Evolution and Adoption

The evolution of AI-driven chatbots has transformed customer interactions. Widespread adoption ensures enhanced engagement.

Significance of ChatGPT in Marketing:
Enhanced Customer Experience
ChatGPT drives personalized interactions. Customer satisfaction ensures loyalty.

24/7 Availability
Automated responses ensure round-the-clock support. Availability drives increased engagement.

ChatGPT in Marketing Applications:
Customer Support and Assistance
Automated responses aid in query resolution. Support ensures seamless customer experiences.

Lead Generation and Qualification
Engaging interactions drive lead qualification. Personalized conversations nurture leads.

Personalized Marketing Campaigns:
Tailored Recommendations
ChatGPT suggests personalized products/services. Recommendations drive conversions.

Interactive Content Distribution
Engaging conversations promote content. Interactions ensure content reach.

ChatGPT for Data Collection and Analysis:
Customer Insights

Conversations offer valuable insights. Data aids in understanding customer behavior.

Analytics and Reporting

Analyzing chat data guides marketing strategies. Insights drive campaign improvements.

Implementing ChatGPT in Marketing:
Chatbot Development

Creating tailored chatbots ensures relevance. Development drives functionality.

Integration with CRM Systems

Syncing chat data aids in customer profiling. Integration enhances marketing strategies.

Challenges in ChatGPT Implementation:
Natural Language Understanding

Interpreting complex queries is challenging. Training ensures accuracy.

Maintaining Human Touch

Balancing automation with personalization is crucial. Conversational tone ensures engagement.

Measuring ChatGPT Success:
Response Time and Accuracy

Efficiency in responses ensures satisfaction. Accuracy guides improvements.

Conversion Rates and Engagement

Analyzing engagement drives marketing success. Conversion metrics ensure effectiveness.

Future Trends in ChatGPT Marketing:
Advanced Personalization

AI-driven personalization ensures relevance. Customization drives engagement.

Multilingual Capabilities

ChatGPT in diverse languages aids global reach. Multilingual support ensures inclusivity.

Conclusion

The integration of ChatGPT technology in marketing strategies signifies a paradigm shift in how agencies engage and interact with their audience. By harnessing personalized experiences, 24/7 availability, lead generation, personalized campaigns, data insights, addressing challenges, measuring success, and exploring future trends, agencies can leverage ChatGPT to enhance marketing effectiveness.

Strategies such as personalized experiences, availability, lead generation, personalized campaigns, data insights, addressing challenges, measuring success, and exploring future trends empower aspiring online agency owners to utilize ChatGPT technology effectively, fostering enhanced engagement and conversion in the ever-evolving marketing landscape.

Section 6: Chapter 3
Mastering Lead Generation with Automation

Lead generation stands as a fundamental pillar in the growth strategy of digital agencies. Embracing automation techniques has revolutionized how businesses generate and nurture leads. This chapter explores the strategic implementation and significant impact of automated lead generation within the realm of digital agencies.

Understanding Automated Lead Generation:
Definition and Mechanisms

Automated lead generation involves using technology to capture, qualify, and nurture leads without manual intervention.

Evolution and Efficiency

Automated systems have evolved lead generation. Efficiency ensures scalability.

The Significance of Automated Lead Generation:
Scalability and Consistency

Automated systems ensure scalability. Consistency drives reliable lead generation.

Enhanced Targeting and Personalization

Automation aids in targeted campaigns. Personalization drives engagement.

Automated Lead Generation Techniques
Landing Pages and Forms

Automated forms ensure lead capture. Landing pages drive conversion.

Email Marketing Automation

Automated email sequences nurture leads. Drip campaigns drive engagement.

Social Media Automation:
Automated Campaigns

Scheduling posts ensures consistent presence. Automation drives engagement.

Data Utilization for Lead Generation:
Analytics and Segmentation

Automated analysis guides targeting. Segmentation ensures tailored approaches.

Predictive Lead Scoring

AI-driven scoring aids in lead prioritization. Predictive analysis ensures quality leads.

Implementing Automated Lead Generation:
CRM Integration
Syncing data aids in lead tracking. Integration ensures effective management.

Marketing Automation Tools
Utilizing specialized tools ensures efficiency. Automation platforms aid execution.

Challenges in Automated Lead Generation:
Data Privacy and Compliance
Adhering to regulations is crucial. Compliance ensures ethical lead generation.

Integration Complexity
Integrating multiple systems is challenging. Streamlining drives efficiency.

Measuring Success in Automated Lead Generation:
Conversion Rates and Quality
Analyzing conversions ensures effectiveness. Quality leads drive sales.

Engagement Metrics
Tracking engagement aids in refining strategies. Interaction ensures interest.

Future Trends in Automated Lead Generation:
AI-Driven Personalization
AI enhances personalized experiences. Customization ensures engagement.

Omni-channel Integration

Utilizing multiple channels aids reach. Integration ensures cohesive strategies.

Conclusion

Automated lead generation techniques have redefined how digital agencies acquire and nurture leads. By harnessing scalability, consistency, targeting, personalization, data utilization, addressing challenges, measuring success, and exploring future trends, agencies can maximize the potential of automated lead generation.

Strategies such as scalability, consistency, targeting, personalization, data utilization, addressing challenges, measuring success, and exploring future trends empower aspiring online agency owners to master lead generation, fostering enhanced engagement and conversion in a dynamic and competitive landscape.

Section 6: Chapter 4
Optimizing Facebook Ads Using Automation Tools

Facebook advertising has emerged as a pivotal tool for digital agencies to reach their target audience effectively. Leveraging automation tools within the Facebook Ads ecosystem has revolutionized advertising strategies. This chapter delves into the strategic implementation and significant impact of automated tools in optimizing Facebook Ads for digital agencies.

Understanding Facebook Ads Automation:
Tools and Capabilities

Automation tools aid in ad creation, targeting, and performance optimization within the Facebook Ads platform.

Evolution and Efficiency Gains

Automated tools have evolved ad strategies. Efficiency ensures precise targeting.

The Significance of Facebook Ads Automation:
Precision Targeting
Automation tools aid in reaching specific demographics. Targeting ensures relevance.

Performance Optimization
Automated optimization drives ad performance. Efficiency enhances ROI.

Automated Tools for Facebook Ads:
Ad Creation and Testing
Automation aids in ad design and copywriting. A/B testing ensures effectiveness.

Audience Targeting
Automated targeting refines audience segments. Precision targeting drives conversions.

Campaign Management Automation:
Budget Allocation
Automated budget management drives efficiency. Optimization ensures ROI.

Performance Monitoring
Automated analytics aid in tracking metrics. Insights guide strategy refinement.

Data Utilization for Optimization:
Insights and Analysis

Automated analysis guides ad optimization. Data utilization ensures targeting precision.

Dynamic Ads Creation
Automation generates personalized ads. Dynamic content ensures engagement.

Implementing Automation in Facebook Ads:
Campaign Structure
Automated setups ensure optimal structures. Frameworks drive performance.

Ad Set and Bidding Optimization
Automation aids in bidding strategies. Optimization ensures cost-effectiveness.

Challenges in Facebook Ads Automation:
Ad Fraud and Quality
Ensuring ad authenticity is crucial. Quality assurance drives trust.

Algorithm Changes
Adapting to platform shifts is challenging. Flexibility ensures adaptability.

Measuring Success in Facebook Ads Automation:
ROI and Conversions
Analyzing returns ensures effectiveness. Conversions drive sales and goals.

Engagement Metrics
Tracking engagement aids in refining strategies. Interaction ensures interest.

Future Trends in Facebook Ads Automation:
AI-Powered Optimization
AI enhances ad performance. Automated optimization ensures efficiency.

Augmented Reality Ads
Interactive ads drive engagement. Innovation ensures user experience.

Conclusion
Facebook Ads automation tools have transformed how digital agencies reach and engage their audience. By harnessing precision targeting, performance optimization, automated tools, campaign management, data utilization, addressing challenges, measuring success, and exploring future trends, agencies can maximize the potential of Facebook Ads for their clients.

Strategies such as precision targeting, performance optimization, automated tools, campaign management, data utilization, addressing challenges, measuring success, and exploring future trends empower aspiring online agency owners to optimize Facebook Ads effectively, driving enhanced engagement and conversions in a competitive digital landscape.

Section 6: Chapter 5
Streamlining Social Media
Automation Strategies

Social media automation has become an integral part of digital agency marketing efforts, allowing efficient management and optimization of social platforms. This chapter delves into the strategic implementation and significant impact of streamlined social media automation strategies for digital agencies.

Understanding Social Media Automation:
Tools and Functions

Automation tools aid in scheduling, posting, and analyzing social media content across various platforms.

Evolution and Efficiency

Automation has evolved social media strategies. Efficiency ensures consistent engagement.

The Significance of Social Media Automation:
Consistent Presence

Automation ensures regular posting schedules. Consistency drives audience engagement.

Audience Engagement

Automated responses drive interaction. Engagement fosters community growth.

Streamlined Social Media Automation Techniques:
Content Scheduling

Automated scheduling ensures timely posts. Consistency drives visibility.

Post Curation and Publication

Automation aids in content discovery. Publishing ensures audience reach.

Automated Response and Engagement:
Chatbot Integration

Automated chatbots drive interaction. Responses ensure continuous engagement.

Comment Moderation

Automated moderation maintains brand integrity. Responses foster community trust.

Data Utilization for Optimization:
Analytics and Insights

Automated analysis guides content strategies. Insights ensure relevant content.

Performance Tracking

Automated metrics aid in strategy refinement. Performance ensures goal alignment.

Implementing Social Media Automation:
Platform Integration

Automated syncing ensures streamlined management. Integration drives efficiency.

Content Calendar and Strategy

Automation aids in content planning. Strategy ensures message consistency.

Challenges in Social Media Automation:
Authenticity and Human Touch

Maintaining genuine interactions is crucial. Personalization ensures engagement.

Algorithm Changes

Adapting to platform shifts is challenging. Flexibility ensures adaptability.

Measuring Success in Social Media Automation
Engagement Metrics

Tracking interaction aids in refining strategies. Engagement ensures audience interest.

Conversion Rates

Analyzing conversions drives effectiveness. Conversions indicate campaign success.

Future Trends in Social Media Automation:

AI-Driven Insights

AI enhances content recommendations. Automated insights ensure relevance.

VR/AR Integration

Innovative content drives engagement. Interactive experiences foster user interest.

Conclusion

Streamlined social media automation strategies have revolutionized how digital agencies manage and engage their audience across platforms. By harnessing consistent presence, audience engagement, streamlined techniques, data utilization, addressing challenges, measuring success, and exploring future trends, agencies can maximize the potential of social media automation.

Strategies such as consistent presence, audience engagement, streamlined techniques, data utilization, addressing challenges, measuring success, and exploring future trends empower aspiring online agency owners to streamline their social media automation, fostering enhanced engagement and community growth in a dynamic digital landscape.

Section 6: Chapter 6
Leveraging AI in Creative Design and Content Creation

Artificial Intelligence (AI) has revolutionized creative design and content creation within the digital landscape. This chapter explores the strategic implementation and significant impact of AI-driven tools in fostering creativity and content creation for digital agencies.

Understanding AI in Creative Design:
AI-Driven Tools

AI-powered tools aid in design creation, image manipulation, and content generation.

Evolution and Innovation

AI has transformed design processes. Innovation ensures creative possibilities.

The Significance of AI in Creative Design:
Efficiency and Speed

AI-driven automation ensures rapid design iterations. Efficiency aids productivity.

Versatility and Innovation

AI fosters diverse design possibilities. Versatility drives creativity.

AI-Powered Tools in Design and Content Creation:
Graphic Design Automation

AI aids in design generation. Templates ensure efficiency and customization.

Image Editing and Enhancement

Automated tools streamline editing processes. Enhancement drives visual appeal.

AI in Content Generation:
Automated Copywriting

AI generates content based on data. Automated copy ensures consistent messaging.

Video Creation and Editing

AI-driven tools aid in video production. Editing ensures engaging content.

Data Utilization for Creative Output:
Predictive Design

AI uses data to predict design preferences. Predictions drive tailored creations.

Analyzing Trends

AI aids in trend analysis. Insights ensure relevant and timely content.

Implementing AI in Creative Processes:
Tool Integration
Automated tools integrate into design workflows. Integration ensures seamless operations.

Workflow Optimization
Automation drives process efficiency. Optimization ensures productive workflows.

Challenges in AI-Driven Creativity:
Authenticity and Originality
Maintaining uniqueness is crucial. Creativity ensures original design elements.

Learning Curve and Expertise
Adapting to AI tools requires expertise. Training ensures effective usage.

Measuring Success in AI-Driven Creativity:
Design Quality Metrics

Analyzing design elements drives effectiveness. Quality ensures visual appeal.

Engagement and Feedback
Tracking audience response aids in content refinement. Engagement ensures relevance.

Future Trends in AI-Driven Creativity:

Enhanced Personalization

AI-driven personalization ensures relevance. Customization drives engagement.

Augmented Reality Integration

Innovative experiences foster engagement. AR/VR ensure immersive content.

Conclusion

Leveraging AI in creative design and content creation marks a paradigm shift in how digital agencies produce compelling visuals and engaging content. By harnessing efficiency gains, versatility, AI-powered tools, content generation, data utilization, addressing challenges, measuring success, and exploring future trends, agencies can maximize the potential of AI in fostering creativity.

Strategies such as efficiency gains, versatility, AI-powered tools, content generation, data utilization, addressing challenges, measuring success, and exploring future trends empower aspiring online agency owners to leverage AI effectively, driving enhanced creativity and content quality in a competitive digital landscape.

Section 6: Chapter 7
Personalization and Targeting with Automated Systems

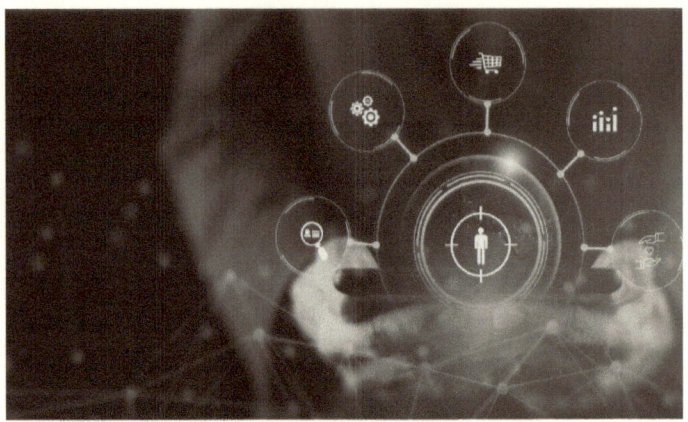

Personalization and precise targeting are paramount in successful digital marketing strategies. Leveraging automated systems for personalized experiences has become crucial in the digital landscape. This chapter explores the strategic implementation and significant impact of automated systems in achieving personalization and precise targeting for digital agencies.

Understanding Personalization and Targeting Automation: Automated Systems Overview

Automated systems utilize data for personalized content delivery and targeted marketing.

Evolution and Precision

Automated systems have evolved marketing strategies. Precision ensures tailored experiences.

The Significance of Personalization and Targeting Automation:
Customer-Centric Approach

Personalization focuses on individual needs. Targeting ensures relevant outreach.

Enhanced User Experience

Tailored experiences drive engagement. User satisfaction ensures brand loyalty.

Automated Systems for Personalization and Targeting:
Customer Profiling and Segmentation

Automated systems categorize audiences. Segmentation ensures personalized targeting.

Dynamic Content Generation

Automated tools produce personalized content. Dynamic content drives engagement.

Personalization in Email Marketing:
Automated Email Campaigns

Personalized emails drive interaction. Automation ensures timely delivery.

Behavior-Driven Targeting

Automated triggers aid in targeting. Behavioral analysis ensures relevance.

Precision Targeting in Advertising:
AI-Driven Ad Optimization

Automated optimization ensures relevance. AI drives efficient targeting.

Retargeting Strategies

Automated retargeting enhances conversions. Precision ensures re-engagement.

Data Utilization for Personalization and Targeting: Predictive Analytics

Automated data analysis aids predictions. Predictions drive personalized strategies.

Real-Time Data Processing

Automation ensures timely insights. Real-time data drives immediate actions.

Implementing Automated Personalization and Targeting CRM Integration

Automated systems sync with customer data. Integration ensures tailored outreach.

Automated Campaign Management

Efficient management drives targeted strategies. Automation ensures seamless execution.

Challenges in Automated Personalization and Targeting: Data Privacy and Ethics

Respecting privacy is crucial. Ethical practices ensure trust and compliance.

Balancing Automation and Human Touch

Maintaining personal connections is vital. Balance ensures genuine interactions.

Measuring Success in Personalization and Targeting: Engagement Metrics

Tracking interaction aids in strategy refinement. Engagement ensures interest.

Conversion Rates and ROI

Analyzing returns ensures effectiveness. Conversions drive campaign success.

Future Trends in Automated Personalization and Targeting Hyper-Personalization

AI-driven personalization ensures relevance. Hyper-personalization drives engagement.

Contextual Targeting

Targeting based on context ensures relevance. Context-driven content fosters engagement.

Conclusion

Automated systems for personalization and targeting have transformed how digital agencies engage and convert their audience. By harnessing a customer-centric approach, enhanced user experiences, automated systems, data utilization, addressing challenges, measuring success, and exploring future trends, agencies can maximize the potential of automation for tailored experiences.

Strategies such as a customer-centric approach, user experiences, automated systems, data utilization, addressing challenges, measuring success, and exploring future trends empower aspiring online agency owners to achieve effective personalization and precise targeting, fostering enhanced engagement and conversions in a competitive digital landscape.

Section 6: Chapter 8
Data-Driven Decision Making in Automation

Data has become the cornerstone of informed decision-making in the realm of automation for digital agencies. This chapter explores the strategic implementation and significant impact of data-driven approaches in making informed decisions within automated systems.

Understanding Data-Driven Decision Making:
Role of Data in Automation

Data serves as the foundation for informed decision-making. Insights guide automation.

Evolution and Influence

Data-driven approaches have revolutionized business strategies. Influence ensures efficiency.

The Significance of Data-Driven Decision Making:

Informed Strategy Formulation

Data insights aid in crafting effective strategies. Informed decisions drive success.

Predictive Capabilities

Data predicts trends and outcomes. Predictions guide future actions.

Data Utilization in Automated Systems:

Analytics and Insights

Automated analytics provide actionable insights. Data utilization ensures optimization.

Predictive Modeling

Automated algorithms aid in predictive analytics. Models guide decision-making.

Automated Systems for Data-Driven Decisions:

AI-Powered Analytics

AI-driven systems analyze vast datasets. Insights drive informed decisions.

Machine Learning Algorithms

Automated learning refines processes. Algorithms ensure optimized actions.

Utilizing Data for Process Optimization:

Workflow Analysis

Data-driven insights streamline operations. Analysis ensures efficiency gains.

Automated Process Enhancement

Data-driven improvements optimize automation. Enhancement ensures performance.

Implementing Data-Driven Decision Making:
Integration of Analytical Tools

Automated systems integrate analytics tools. Integration aids informed decisions.

AI-Based Decision Support

AI systems aid decision-making processes. Support ensures accuracy.

Challenges in Data-Driven Decision Making:
Data Quality and Interpretation

Ensuring data accuracy is crucial. Interpretation ensures meaningful insights.

Ethical Use of Data

Respecting privacy is essential. Ethical practices build trust.

Measuring Success in Data-Driven Automation:
Performance Metrics

Tracking metrics ensures effectiveness. Performance drives optimization.

ROI and Business Impact

Analyzing returns guides decision effectiveness. Impact ensures goal alignment.

Future Trends in Data-Driven Automation:

Advanced Predictive Analytics

AI enhances predictive capabilities. Advanced analytics drive insights.

Augmented Decision-Making Tools

Tools aid human decision-makers. Augmentation ensures informed choices.

Conclusion

Data-driven decision-making is pivotal in leveraging automation for digital agencies. By harnessing data insights, informed strategy formulation, data utilization, addressing challenges, measuring success, and exploring future trends, agencies can maximize the potential of data-driven approaches within automated systems.

Strategies such as data insights, strategy formulation, data utilization, addressing challenges, measuring success, and exploring future trends empower aspiring online agency owners to make informed decisions, fostering enhanced efficiency and performance in a competitive digital landscape.

Section 6: Chapter 9
Integrating Automation into
Marketing Workflows

The seamless integration of automation into marketing workflows has become fundamental in enhancing efficiency and productivity for digital agencies. This chapter explores the strategic implementation and significant impact of integrating automation within marketing workflows.

Understanding Automation Integration in Marketing:
Role of Automation

Automation streamlines marketing processes. Integration drives efficiency gains.

Evolution and Influence

Integrated automation has transformed marketing strategies. Influence ensures optimization.

The Significance of Automation Integration:
Workflow Efficiency

Integration ensures streamlined processes. Efficiency drives productivity.

Scalability and Consistency

Automated workflows ensure scalability. Consistency aids reliable performance.

Automation Tools in Marketing Workflows:
CRM and Marketing Automation

Integrated systems aid in customer management. Automation ensures targeted campaigns.

Email Marketing Automation

Automated sequences enhance engagement. Integration ensures workflow continuity.

Social Media Management:
Automated Publishing and Monitoring

Integrated tools schedule posts. Automation aids in audience engagement.

Community Management

Automated responses foster community growth. Integration ensures brand consistency.

Content Creation and Distribution:
Automated Content Creation

Integrated tools aid in content generation. Automation ensures diverse content.

Distribution and Analytics

Integrated systems streamline content distribution. Analytics guide strategy refinement.

Implementing Integrated Automation:
Workflow Mapping

Mapping processes aids in integration. Integration ensures seamless workflows.

Tool Selection and Integration

Choosing and integrating tools drives efficiency. Integration ensures functionality.

Challenges in Automation Integration:
Compatibility and Synchronization

Ensuring system compatibility is crucial. Synchronization ensures workflow continuity.

Adaptation and Training

Adapting to new systems requires training. Skill development drives usage efficiency.

Measuring Success in Automation Integration:
Workflow Optimization Metrics

Tracking efficiency gains ensures effectiveness. Optimization drives productivity.

ROI and Resource Utilization

Analyzing returns guides investment. Resource utilization ensures efficiency.

Future Trends in Automation Integration:
AI-Powered Integration
AI enhances system cohesion. Integrated AI ensures streamlined workflows.

Unified Marketing Platforms
Integrated platforms drive seamless operations. Unified systems ensure workflow continuity.

Conclusion
Integration of automation into marketing workflows is pivotal for digital agencies. By harnessing workflow efficiency, scalability, integrated tools, addressing challenges, measuring success, and exploring future trends, agencies can maximize the potential of integrated automation in marketing.

Strategies such as workflow efficiency, scalability, integrated tools, addressing challenges, measuring success, and exploring future trends empower aspiring online agency owners to integrate automation effectively, fostering enhanced productivity and performance in a competitive digital landscape.

Section 6: Chapter 10
Future Trends and Innovations in Digital Business Automation

The landscape of digital business automation continues to evolve, promising innovative trends that will redefine the way online agencies operate. This chapter explores emerging trends and innovations expected to shape the future of digital business automation.

Understanding Future Trends in Digital Business Automation: Role of Innovation

Innovation drives evolution in digital automation. Future trends redefine processes.

Anticipated Impact

Future trends promise enhanced efficiency and productivity. Impact ensures competitiveness.

The Paradigm of AI and Machine Learning:
Advanced AI Integration

AI-driven automation revolutionizes workflows. Integration ensures enhanced decision-making.

Machine Learning Algorithms

Continuous learning enhances systems. Algorithms drive adaptive automation.

Hyper-Personalization and Customer-Centric Automation:
Contextual Personalization

Automation tailors experiences based on context. Personalization ensures engagement.

Predictive Customer Journeys

Automation predicts user behaviors. Predictions guide customized experiences.

Robotic Process Automation (RPA) Advancements:
Cognitive Automation

RPA integrates cognitive capabilities. Automation ensures complex task handling.

Autonomous Processes

Self-learning automation enhances workflows. Autonomy drives efficiency gains.

Blockchain Technology Integration:
Transparent Automation

Blockchain ensures data integrity. Integration fosters trust in automated systems.

Smart Contracts and Workflow Automation

Automated contracts drive streamlined processes. Smart contracts ensure reliability.

Quantum Computing's Role in Automation:
Enhanced Computational Power

Quantum computing drives data processing. Power ensures rapid automation.

Optimization of Complex Algorithms

Automation leverages complex algorithms. Optimization drives efficiency gains.

Augmented Reality (AR) and Virtual Reality (VR) Integration:
Immersive Experiences

AR/VR redefine user interactions. Integration ensures enhanced engagement.

Training and Simulation Automation

Automated simulations aid in training. Automation ensures realistic experiences.

Cybersecurity Automation:
Automated Threat Detection

Automation detects and responds to threats. Security ensures system integrity.

AI-Powered Security Measures

AI-driven defenses enhance protection. Automation safeguards digital assets.

Environmental Sustainability Through Automation:

Green Automation Practices

Automated systems prioritize eco-friendly operations. Sustainability drives responsibility.

Resource Optimization

Automation optimizes resource utilization. Efficiency ensures sustainability.

Conclusion

The future of digital business automation holds promising advancements. Embracing trends such as AI integration, hyper-personalization, RPA advancements, blockchain technology, quantum computing, AR/VR integration, cybersecurity automation, and environmental sustainability ensures that digital agencies remain at the forefront of innovation.

Strategies such as embracing innovation, AI integration, hyper-personalization, RPA advancements, blockchain technology, quantum computing, AR/VR integration, cybersecurity automation, and environmental sustainability empower aspiring online agency owners to prepare for future trends, fostering continued growth and adaptability in an ever-evolving digital landscape.

Digital Agency Blueprint
10 Steps to Launch and Grow Your Online Empire

Step 1: Define Your Niche and Services

Identify your area of expertise, whether it's social media marketing, web design, SEO, content creation, etc.

Action: Utilize insights from Chapter 1 to understand the digital business landscape and select a specialized area aligned with your skills and market demand.

Step 2: Conduct Market Research and Plan

Research your target audience, competitors, and market trends.

Action: Use Chapter 2 to conduct thorough market research, identify opportunities, and craft a comprehensive business plan outlining your goals, USP, and strategies.

Step 3: Implement Automated Tools and Systems

Integrate automation tools for efficiency and productivity.

Action: Apply lessons from Chapters 3 and 4 to implement tools for CRM, social media automation, content creation, and analytics to streamline processes.

Step 4: Develop a Strong Brand and Positioning

Create a recognizable brand identity and position your agency uniquely.

Action: Utilize Chapter 9's insights to integrate automation into your marketing workflows and establish a consistent brand presence across platforms.

Step 5: Build and Manage a Strong Team

Recruit, train, and manage a skilled team to support your agency.

Action: Apply lessons from Chapters 5 to 8 to automate HR processes, foster a positive company culture, and leverage automation in training and skill development.

Step 6: Scale and Expand Services

Expand services, innovate, and adapt to industry changes.

Action: Use Chapter 10's future trend insights to prepare for advancements, scale services, and leverage emerging technologies like AI, VR, blockchain, etc., for innovative offerings.

Step 7: Continuous Learning and Improvement

Embrace a culture of learning and continuous improvement.

Action: Apply insights from Chapters 7 and 8 to make data-driven decisions, optimize workflows, and foster innovation within your agency.

Step 8: Ensure Ethical Practices and Sustainability

Prioritize ethical business practices and sustainability.

Action: Implement lessons from Chapter 10 to integrate sustainable practices and ensure ethical use of automation tools within your agency.

Step 9: Network and Collaborate

Network with industry experts and collaborate for growth opportunities.

Action: Leverage your expertise and connections, as highlighted in Chapter 9, to collaborate with other agencies or influencers for mutual growth.

Step 10: Measure Success and Adapt

Monitor performance metrics and adapt to changing trends.

Action: Apply Chapter 8's data-driven decision-making principles to measure success, analyze metrics, and adapt strategies for continual growth.

Final Note:

Starting an online digital agency is an ongoing journey filled with opportunities for innovation, adaptation, and continual growth. To succeed in this dynamic landscape, consider the following key points:

- **Adaptability is Key:** The digital realm is constantly evolving. Embrace change and stay agile to adapt your strategies, tools, and services to meet evolving industry and consumer needs.

- **Continuous Learning:** Commit to lifelong learning. Stay updated with industry trends, attend webinars, workshops, and engage in professional development to expand your expertise continually.

- **Client-Centric Approach:** Prioritize client satisfaction and build long-term relationships. Understand and address their needs with personalized, value-driven solutions.

- **Data is Your Compass:** Utilize data-driven insights to steer your agency's direction. Regularly analyze metrics, customer feedback, and market trends to refine strategies and make informed decisions.

- **Innovation and Creativity:** Foster a culture of innovation within your agency. Encourage creativity among your team to explore new ideas, technologies, and solutions that set you apart.

- **Collaboration and Partnerships:** Network extensively within the industry. Collaborate with other agencies, industry experts, or influencers to amplify your reach, learn from others, and explore new opportunities.

- **Ethics and Responsibility:** Uphold ethical practices in all aspects of your business. Build trust and credibility by maintaining integrity, respecting data privacy, and practicing responsible automation.

- **Resilience and Perseverance:** Understand that challenges are part of the journey. Stay resilient, learn from setbacks, and use them as opportunities to grow stronger.
- **Celebrate Milestones:** Recognize and celebrate your agency's achievements, both big and small. Acknowledge the efforts of your team and use successes as motivation for continued progress.

Action: Use these steps as a roadmap, continually refine your strategies, and stay updated with the latest trends to thrive in the competitive digital business landscape.

From The Author

Congratulations on completing "From Idea to Empire: Mastering the Online Agency Game."

This journey through the intricacies of establishing and flourishing in the realm of digital agencies has equipped you with invaluable insights, strategies, and a roadmap for success.

As you conclude this book, remember that the culmination of knowledge and guidance within these pages is merely the beginning of your entrepreneurial venture. The path you embark upon is dynamic, filled with challenges, opportunities, and continuous evolution.

Keep in mind these key takeaways:

- **Action is the Catalyst:** Implementation is pivotal. Apply the knowledge gained here into tangible actions within your digital agency. Experiment, adapt, and refine strategies based on your unique circumstances and market dynamics.
- **Embrace Innovation:** Innovation drives progress. Stay attuned to emerging technologies, trends, and consumer behaviors. Be the architect of change within your agency, leveraging innovation to stay ahead in the competitive digital landscape.
- **Persistence Pays Off:** Building an online empire is a journey that demands perseverance. Embrace challenges as learning opportunities, stay resilient, and maintain focus on your long-term goals.

- **Continual Growth:** Growth is not just about scaling your agency but also personal and professional development. Embrace continuous learning, seek mentorship, and foster a growth mindset to propel both yourself and your agency forward.

Remember, success is not merely the attainment of a goal, but a continuous pursuit of excellence and evolution.

As you venture forth, may the lessons from this book serve as a compass guiding you through the complexities and opportunities of the digital business landscape. Take bold strides, innovate fearlessly, and create your unique mark in the ever-expanding world of online agencies.

Wishing you boundless success in your journey to build and nurture your digital empire!

Best regards,

Aniket More